Editor's ToolKit Plus 2023™

Editor's ToolKit Plus 2023™

Jack Lyon

THE EDITORIUM™

This book's page layout was done with the Editorium's BookMaker add-in. The index was produced with DEXembed and DEXter. You can learn more at www.editorium.com

ISBN 978-1-4341-0494-6

The Editorium
West Jordan, UT 84081-6132
www.editorium.com
editor@editorium.com

Contents

Introduction

What is Editor's ToolKit Plus?

Editor's ToolKit Plus is a Microsoft Word add-in, a comprehensive suite of editing tools that run inside Microsoft Word. In order of their appearance on the ribbon interface:

- *Editor's ToolKit* (without the "Plus") is a collection of basic tools designed for detailed line editing, making it easy to work with *revisions, formatting, navigation, documents,* and *text.*
- *FileCleaner* cleans up common mechanical problems such as multiple spaces, multiple returns, straight quotation marks, unnecessary formatting, and so on.
- *NoteStripper* turns Word's embedded notes into regular text, or vice versa.
- *ListFixer* turns Word's bulleted and numbered formatting into actual bullets and numbers, or vice versa.
- *MegaReplacer* finds and replaces multiple items (such as common misspellings) in multiple files, all at the same time.

- *Puller* pulls out parenthetical items, bracketed items, comments, revisions, citations, index entries, and much more, and puts them into a new document for your review.
- *WordCounter* counts the number of words in the active document, all open documents, or all documents in a folder. It can also give you an alphabetical list of those words with a count of how often they appear.
- *Switcheroo* automatically switches the current word with a different word as specified by you in an easy-to-use table.
- *QuoteMe* turns block quotations into regular text quotations or vice versa and adjusts internal quotation marks as needed.
- *Converters* convert Microsoft Word documents into other formats, such as ePub, LaTeX, Markdown, QuarkConverter, and InDesign.
- *Projects* saves all open Microsoft Word documents as a named project, which will later open those documents automatically when you open the project.
- *Research* automatically looks up selected text in a variety of online reference works.
- *MacroVault* gives you an easy-to-use interface and custom keyboard shortcuts for your own collection of custom macros.

I originally created Editor's ToolKit Plus to lighten the workload of the editors at the publishing house where I worked. Since then, I've expanded and refined the program to better meet my own needs as well as the stated needs of many other editors and publishers. Those needs include (in order):

- Document cleanup.
- Working with styles.
- Editing text.
- Creating documents that can be imported cleanly into typesetting programs like InDesign and QuarkXPress.

In other words, Editor's ToolKit Plus addresses the entire editing process, from raw manuscript to edited document ready for design and typesetting.

Why should I use Editor's ToolKit Plus?

Editor's ToolKit Plus will make your work easier and *save you time.* If you're on salary, that will make your employer happy. If you're self-employed, and you charge by the project, the page, or the number of words, you can increase your earnings per hour by increasing your efficiency. Editor's ToolKit Plus makes it possible to do more—a *lot* more—in the time you have available. For example, you could spend a couple of hours properly title-casing document headings, making sure that articles, conjunctions, and prepositions are correctly lowercased. Or, you could have Editor's ToolKit Plus do it for you in less than a minute. If you're charging $500 to edit that document, you just freed up two hours that you can use to edit, say, a $200 document. That means you're making more money in the same amount of time. The more hours you can free up, the more you're actually making per hour.

What are some of the most useful features?

All of the features are useful, of course, but here are some that I use most often:

Customized keyboard shortcuts

Editor's ToolKit Plus includes many customized keyboard shortcuts designed specifically for editing. One of my favorites, surprising in its simplicity, is pressing CTRL DELETE to delete a word. That's already a feature in Microsoft Word, of course, but Word requires you to put your cursor in *front* of the word before deleting. With

Editor's ToolKit Plus, you can put your cursor *anywhere* in the word you want to delete. Then press CTRL DELETE to make it go away. Over the course of editing a manuscript, that will save you *thousands* of keystrokes, especially considering that deleting unnecessary words is a big part of editing.

Other shortcut keys make it a cinch to transpose words, transpose characters, capitalize words, lowercase words, italicize words, and so on, with a single keystroke. These shortcuts are not completely arbitrary; I've tried to arrange them so that the most common editorial tasks are right at your fingertips. For example, F7 toggles italic on and off. Yes, CTRL I does the same thing, but after you've used F7 a few times, CTRL I will seem clunky and annoying. Something that small does make a difference in how easily and smoothly you're able to work.

A couple of other favorite keyboard shortcuts:

Press F9 to title-case the current word and automatically jump to the next word.

Press F10 to lowercase the current word and automatically jump to the next word.

Using those two keys, you can merrily hop from word to word, title-casing and lowercasing as needed. To really appreciate how slick this is, you need to try it for yourself.

Title-case selected text

But maybe you'd rather title-case a whole string of words, properly and automatically, without having to decide how to treat each one. If so, try another of my favorites, *Title-case selected text.* To use it, select the text you want to be in title case and (as above) press F9. The selected words will be title-cased.

But doesn't Microsoft Word already have that feature? Well, sort of. Take this example:

The call of the wild

Microsoft Word turns it (incorrectly) into this:

The Call Of The Wild

Editor's ToolKit Plus turns it (correctly) into this:

The Call of the Wild

In other words, Editor's ToolKit Plus properly handles common articles, conjunctions, and prepositions. It also title-cases the first and last words of your selection, and it title-cases any word following a colon, as specified in most style guides.

Batch processing

That brings us to batch processing, the most powerful feature in the program. If I have forty chapters to edit, with each chapter in a separate document, I can use *Title-case headings* to properly title-case *all* of the headings in *all* of those chapters at the same time, and I can do that with just a few clicks of the mouse. Many of the features in Editor's ToolKit Plus include batch processing, working on your choice of the active document, all open documents, or all documents in a folder.

FileCleaner

One of those batch-processing features is FileCleaner, which automatically cleans up some of the most common problems in electronic manuscripts, including:

- Multiple spaces in a row.
- Multiple returns in a row.
- Spaces around returns.
- Double hyphens that should be em dashes.
- Hyphens between numbers that should be en dashes.
- Straight quotation marks that should be curly quotation marks.

And much, much more. These are the kinds of picky little problems you might fix with Word's Find and Replace feature, but you'd have to handle each problem separately, and you'd have to do so in each chapter separately. Using FileCleaner, you can quickly and easily fix multiple problems in multiple documents.

Cleaning up these mechanical problems—*before* substantive editing—makes substantive editing much easier. When the mechanical problems are gone, my brain doesn't have to deal with them. If I *don't* clean them up before editing, every time I come to a double space between sentences, my brain sees it and wants to fix it. That's just a tiny distraction, but when those distractions keep popping up, they make it difficult to focus on more substantial problems. FileCleaner gets them out of the way.

FileCleaner also cleans up various problems with formatting. For example, the option to "remove font format overrides (but preserve bold, italic, etc.)" removes all those unnecessary, inconsistent fonts that authors like to use to "prettify" their text, but at the same time it leaves formatting like italic, bold, and superscript intact, along with styles. You won't believe what a difference this makes in cleaning up a manuscript.

MegaReplacer

FileCleaner is great for cleaning up mechanical problems, but what if you have other problems that you need to clean up? What if you need to go through three dozen documents and change *millenium* to *millennium*, along with dozens of other misspellings (*supercede* to *supersede, rarify* to *rarefy,* and so on)? That's what MegaReplacer is for. Again, it works on the active document, all open documents, or all documents in a folder. But unlike FileCleaner, it allows you to define your *own* find-and-replace items and then run them *en masse*. To get you started, MegaReplacer comes with a long list of corrections ("Automatic corrections for MegaReplacer.docx") that you can use as is or modify to meet your needs.

Using that list with MegaReplacer makes it possible to fix multiple misspellings in multiple documents *without* tediously running Word's spell-checker. The spell-checker is a terrific tool for finding random typographical errors, but if you're using it to find common misspellings, you'll need to okay, replace, or ignore each misspelling manually—a colossal waste of time. After all, you already *know* they're misspellings; why not fix them all in one go? Let MegaReplacer correct any possible occurrences while you take a break or work on something else. If you want to catch typos, run the spell-checker *after* fixing misspellings with MegaReplacer, and you'll have far fewer errors to deal with.

Similarly, the PerfectIt add-in from Intelligent Editing is wonderful, and you should definitely use it to ensure consistency. But if you already know that your house style specifies, say, *healthcare* rather than *health care,* you don't need PerfectIt to point out deviations. Just use MegaReplacer to fix them all. *Then* use PerfectIt to find other inconsistencies that might not be on your radar.

How can I learn more?

The best way to learn about the features in Editor's ToolKit Plus is to use them. Look through this manual and read about the features that look interesting. Then try them out on some junk documents. The 45-day evaluation period gives you plenty of time.

I use Editor's ToolKit Plus all the time in my own work. It makes that work easier and faster, and I can't imagine editing without it. I hope you find it as useful as I do.

Note: **The features described in this manual can be found on the Editor's ToolKit Plus ribbon under the menu button that corresponds with the chapter in the manual. For example, "Remove highlighting," covered in the "Text" chapter, is under the "Text" menu on the ribbon. Many features, such as FileCleaner, NoteStripper, Converters, Projects, and Research, have their own menu button and their own chapter.**

Getting Started

The first item on the program's ribbon interface is Editor's ToolKit Plus. Click the icon to see the various options for running Editor's ToolKit Plus:

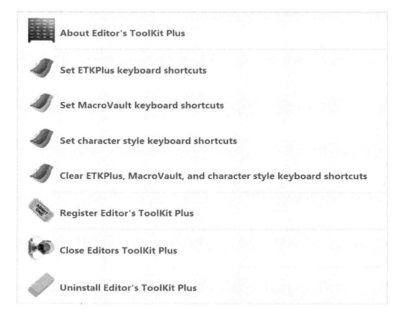

About Editor's ToolKit Plus

Set ETKPlus keyboard shortcuts

Set MacroVault keyboard shortcuts

Set character style keyboard shortcuts

Clear ETKPlus, MacroVault, and character style keyboard shortcuts

Register Editor's ToolKit Plus

Close Editors ToolKit Plus

Uninstall Editor's ToolKit Plus

About Editor's ToolKit Plus

This feature gives you the version number of the program. It also tells you if you've registered the program by purchasing a license to use it and then entered your password/registration code to keep the program from timing out:

Set ETKPlus keyboard shortcuts

This feature sets custom keyboard shortcuts that help turn Microsoft Word into an editing environment rather than a general office setup, making a big difference in efficiency. If you activate these shortcuts and later change your mind, you can always deactivate them and go back to Word's defaults. (See "Clear ETKPlus, MacroVault, and character style keyboard shortcuts" below.)

To see exactly what all of the custom shortcuts are, see appendix 1, "Keyboard Shortcuts." The shortcuts are also listed in *ETKPlus 2023 keyboard template.docx*, which you should find on your desktop after installing the program.

Please note that these keyboard shortcuts may take precedence over some of your own shortcuts, so if your regular shortcuts now do something else, that's why. But please don't worry. If you close Editor's ToolKit Plus or deactivate its shortcuts, your original shortcuts will remain intact.

PAGE DOWN and PAGE UP keys

In Word, you can Set *View > Zoom* to show one page at a time:

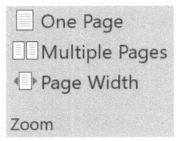

Then, if the Editor's ToolKit Plus custom keyboard shortcuts are active, the PAGE DOWN and PAGE UP keys always go to the *top* of the page (like turning a paper manuscript page) rather than the next screen. This makes a real difference in the "feel" of editing on the computer, especially if you have a big monitor or one that can be pivoted to portrait rather than landscape orientation.

Keys for special characters

The custom keyboard shortcuts also make it possible to insert em dashes, en dashes, and bullets with simple key combinations. No more picking your way through Word's symbol charts!

- SHIFT F2 for an em dash.
- SHIFT F3 for an en dash.
- SHIFT F4 for a bullet (followed by a space).

Creating custom keyboard shortcuts for ETKPlus features

If you don't want to use the keyboard shortcuts for Editor's ToolKit Plus, you may still be able to create your own shortcuts to activate the features listed in *Keybtemp.docx* (the Editor's ToolKit keyboard template). Here's how:

1. Click *View > Macros > Record Macro* (under the little arrow).
2. Give your macro a name.
3. Click the *Keyboard* button
4. Enter the keyboard shortcut you want to use. If it's already in use, Word will tell you so, in which case you can reassign it to your macro or try a different shortcut.
5. Click the *Assign* button (on PC) or the *OK* button (on Macintosh).
6. Click the *Close* button (on PC).
7. Run one of the features in Editor's ToolKit Plus.
8. Click *View > Macros > Stop Recording* (under the little arrow).

Then, when you press your custom keyboard shortcut, the macro you recorded should run the feature in Editor's ToolKit Plus. If the feature *doesn't* run, it's probably not possible to assign that feature to a custom keyboard shortcut.

Set MacroVault keyboard shortcuts

Sets custom keyboard shortcuts for your personal macros displayed in MacroVault. See the "MacroVault" section for more information.

Set character style keyboard shortcuts

Directly applied formatting (such as bold and italic) will be lost when a document is imported into a typesetting program like Adobe InDesign. The solution is to use bold and italic character styles rather than directly applied formatting. The problem is, there's no easy, effective way to do that in Microsoft Word. But if you use Editor's ToolKit Plus to set character style keyboard shortcuts, when you press CTRL I you'll get an *Italic* character style, not just italic formatting. When you press CTRL B, you'll get a **Bold** character style. When you use CTRL I and then CTRL B on the same text, you'll get a ***Bold Italic*** character style. Select some text, press CTRL I, then CTRL B, then CTRL U, and you'll get ***Bold Italic Underline***—all in a single character style. Press CTRL I again, and the italic will be *removed,* leaving just a **Bold Underline** character style. (Yes, these shortcuts are toggles, just like Word's default formatting keys!) All of this happens automatically and transparently if you use this feature.

Note: None of this affects formatting that you do with the mouse; it works with keyboard shortcuts *only.* Also, these shortcuts will not work in Word's Find/Replace dialog because they now activate character styles rather than directly applied formatting. To search for character styles in the Find/Replace dialog, click the *More* button and then click *Format > Styles.* To search for directly applied formatting, click the *More* button and then click *Format > Font.*

Here are the keyboard shortcuts to apply character styles, most of which are the same as Word's defaults for applying font formatting:

CTRL B	Bold
CTRL I *or* F7	Italic
CTRL U	Underline
CTRL /	Strikethrough
F6	Small caps

CTRL +	Subscript
CTRL SHIFT +	Superscript

Clear ETKPlus, MacroVault, and character style keyboard shortcuts

If you activate the custom keyboard shortcuts but later decide you'd rather use Word's defaults, you can use this feature, which clears all of the custom keyboard shortcuts you have set with Editor's ToolKit Plus, including the shortcuts for MacroVault and applying character styles. However, any custom keyboard shortcuts you've created on your own will be left intact. To turn the shortcuts back on, click the menu items for those you want to use.

NOTE: From this point on, the program documentation will assume that the custom ETKPlus keyboard shortcuts are active.

Register Editor's ToolKit Plus

Allows you to enter your password/registration key to keep the program from timing out. You'll receive the password by email when you purchase a license to use the program. For more information, see the "Registration" section toward the end of this document.

Close Editor's ToolKit Plus

Closes Editor's ToolKit Plus and restores Microsoft Word to its original "general user" configuration. This deactivates all of the program's features and shortcut keys.

Restart Editor's ToolKit Plus

To restart Editor's ToolKit Plus, simply restart Microsoft Word.

Uninstall Editor's ToolKit Plus

Uninstalls Editor's ToolKit Plus so it is no longer available as a Microsoft Word add-in. You'll need to use this feature before installing a new version.

Check for updates

The program automatically checks for updates when you start Microsoft Word or Editor's ToolKit Plus. If an update is available, the program notifies you and asks if you'd like to download it. You'll never need to wonder if you have the most recent version.

Editor's Toolkit

Editor's ToolKit (without the powerful "Plus" features) provides basic tools for detailed line editing, including the ability to quickly transpose words, transpose characters, change case, insert dashes and bullets, and much more. I created it because, in all my years of editing, I could never find a word processor designed specifically for editors. Finally I decided to make one, using Microsoft Word as a foundation. I chose Word because it already includes so many useful features for editors and, with its programming language, is designed to be customized. Also, Word is already widely used in the publishing industry, making it a natural choice.

In writing these instructions, I'm assuming you already know how to use Microsoft Word. If you don't, please learn to do so before trying to use Editor's ToolKit. (See appendix 2, "Word Functions for Editors.") This documentation is not intended to take the place of Word manuals and Help files or even to explain Word's functions.

Using the keyboard template

Part of what makes Editor's ToolKit easy to use is the fact that the most frequently accessed functions are available on the program's shortcut keys, so you can use the program without reaching for the mouse all the time. I *strongly* recommend that you learn and use these keys. To remind you of what the keys do, Editor's ToolKit comes with a keyboard template that you can place above the function keys on your keyboard. The template comes in a document called *ETKPlus 2023 keyboard template.docx.* To use it:

1. Open ETKPlus 2023 keyboard template.docx in Word.
2. Print the template.
3. Cut off the excess paper below the bottom line of the template. (For durability, you could print the template on card stock and laminate it.)
4. Place the template above the function keys on your keyboard (F1, F2, etc.). (You may want to tape the template in place.)

The bottom line on the template lists the functions that can be accessed simply by pressing the function keys, and these are the functions you'll probably use most often. To use the functions on the next line up, hold down the SHIFT key while pressing the function keys. You can access the functions on the third line up by holding down the CTRL key, and those on the top line by holding down CTRL SHIFT. For more information, see appendix 1, "Keyboard Shortcuts."

Features of Editor's ToolKit

I've made the program's most frequently used features accessible from the keyboard. Most of them are also accessible from the menus in the Editor's ToolKit group in the ribbon at the top of the screen. Many of the features are self-explanatory. This documentation covers mainly those that aren't, following (mostly) the order in which the features appear on the ribbon.

Editing with Editor's ToolKit

Ordinarily, when I edit a document with Editor's ToolKit, I follow this procedure:

1. I back up my documents so I'll have the originals to go back to if the need arises.
2. I use *Document > Prepare documents for editing* to apply the *Typespec* template.
3. I use FileCleaner to clean up all kinds of common typographical and editorial problems.
4. I apply paragraph styles to headings, block quotations, and so on.
5. I again use the *Document > Prepare documents for editing* feature to lock pages and turn on revision tracking.
6. I edit the documents, using the various features of Editor's ToolKit and Microsoft Word. I especially use the features that are accessible with the function keys, such as capping and lowercasing words, transposing words and characters, italicizing words, showing and stetting revisions, and so on. The customized function keys make all of these features a true pleasure to use.
7. I use the Finish Edited Documents feature to unlock pages, turn off revision marking, make revisions permanent, and prepare the documents for typesetting in Adobe InDesign or other page layout programs.

For me, Editor's ToolKit makes line editing fast, easy, and efficient. I hope you enjoy it as much as I do.

Batch Processing

Many features of Editor's ToolKit Plus include batch processing. For example, if you run WordCounter, you'll see a dialog that lets you use the feature with the active document, all open documents, or all documents in a folder:

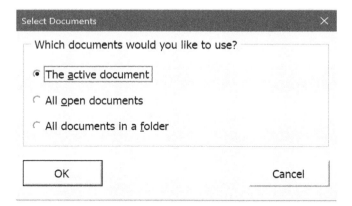

Other features, such as FileCleaner and MegaReplacer, offer even more options, allowing you to specify text ranges and revision tracking:

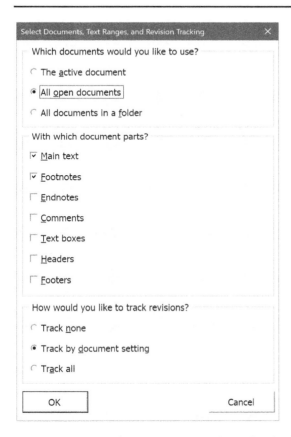

The main point of all this, especially with FileCleaner and MegaReplacer, is to clean up definite problems and inconsistencies in a manuscript *before* you start editing, which means you won't have to deal with those problems and inconsistencies *while* you are editing. If you're also using PerfectIt to deal with those things (which you should be), there will be fewer things you'll need to check while running PerfectIt because you've already fixed so many of them with FileCleaner and MegaReplacer.

Text ranges

You can use any of these text ranges:

- Main text.
- Footnotes.
- Endnotes.
- Comments.
- Text boxes.
- Headers.
- Footers.

But be sure to choose only the text ranges you actually need. Otherwise, the program will take longer to run because it's going through text ranges unnecessarily. For example, you usually won't need to work on comments, headers, and footers, but if you need to, you can. For documents without footnotes or endnotes, the main text may be all you need to use. Be sure to choose at least *one* of these options; otherwise, the program will run but nothing in your documents will be changed.

Revision tracking

You can also choose how you'd like to track revisions. You can:

- *Track none.* If you select this option, the program will *not* track revisions, even if tracking in the document was originally turned on.
- *Track by document setting.* With this option, if revision tracking is turned on in a document, the program will correctly track revisions, even with wildcard searches. If, on the other hand, revision tracking is turned *off* in a document, the program will *not* track revisions.

- *Track all.* If you select this option, the program *will* correctly track revisions, even with wildcard searches, and even if tracking in the document was originally turned off.

If you need to turn revision tracking on or off for multiple documents at once, you can do so by clicking *Revisions > Set revision tracking in multiple documents.*

How revision tracking works with batch processing

A longstanding bug in Microsoft Word causes problems if you're using wildcard searches while also tracking revisions. You can see this for yourself with the following test:

1. Create a new document.
2. Type the following text into the document:

      2-4

4. Turn on revision tracking (track changes).
5. Press CTRL H to display Word's Replace dialog.
6. In the Find what box, enter this:

      ([0-9])-([0-9])

That wildcard string tells Word to find any number followed by a hyphen followed by any number.

7. In the "Replace with" box, enter this:

      \2-\1

That tells Word to replace the first number with the second, enter a hyphen, and replace the second number with the first.

8. If it's available, click the *More* button.
9. Put a check in the box labeled "Use wildcards"
10. Click *Replace all.*

The result *should* be this:

> 4-2

But instead, with revision tracking turned on, the result is this:

> 42-

That's a simple example; many features of Editor's ToolKit Plus, notably FileCleaner, use much more complicated wildcard searches, which could make a real mess while tracking revisions. To work around this problem, FileCleaner and other features don't track revisions while making changes. Instead, they track revisions *after* making changes by using this procedure:

1. Create a temporary document.
2. Insert the text from the real document into the temporary document.
3. Work on the real document with tracking turned off.
4. Compare the temporary document with the real document.

The result is tracked revisions in the real document without the problems caused by using revisions with wildcard searches. That means you can use wildcard searches in MegaReplacer and in your macros in MacroVault and still correctly track revisions when using batch processing.

Revisions

Set revision tracking in active document

Set revision tracking in multiple documents

Show revisions

Stet selected revisions

Review revisions

Accept all revisions

Reject all revisions

Count revisions

Show comments

Microsoft Word can keep track of your revisions with colored strikeouts (for deletions) and underlining (for insertions)—the perfect feature for professional editing because it lets you see the changes you've made, just as if you were editing on paper.

Set revision tracking in the active document (toggle)

Editor's ToolKit gives you two convenient ways to set revision tracking in the active document:

- F2 Key (toggle)
- Revisions > Track revisions (toggle)

Set revision tracking in multiple documents

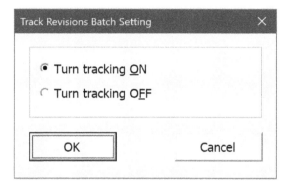

You can also turn revision tracking on or off in the active document, all open documents, or all documents in a folder.

Show and stet revisions

Unfortunately, Word has no easy, natural way to let you see and review all of your revisions at once or to easily and selectively undo them. Editor's ToolKit fixes this problem, letting you see revisions at the touch of a key (F4). Then you can put your cursor on a revision, press the Stet key (F3), and watch the revision go back to the way it was. You can also select whole sections and stet them. Another keystroke (F4), and your revisions are hidden again. Of course, you can work with revisions hidden (my preference) or with revisions showing. For your convenience, showing revisions also lets you view hidden characters, such as spaces and carriage returns.

- F4 key to show or hide revisions (toggle)
- F3 to stet revisions
- Revisions > Show revisions (toggle)
- Revisions > Stet selected revisions

Review revisions

Reviewing revisions is actually rather cumbersome in Word. First, you must use the mouse to click the *Previous* and *Next* icons on the *Review* tab of the Ribbon, when using keyboard shortcuts would be much easier. Second, whether the text is marked for insertion or deletion, it's still *there* on the screen. And to make it go away (or to retain it) requires a *different* action for an insertion than it does for a deletion—and therein lies the problem.

Consider: To *remove* inserted text, you must *reject* the revision. To *retain* inserted text, you must *accept* the revision.

Conversely, to *remove* deleted text, you must *accept* the revision. To *retain* deleted text, you must *reject* the revision.

How confusing! Here's a grid that shows what happens:

Revision Type	Accept	Reject
Insertion	Text retained	Text removed
Deletion	Text removed	Text retained

When reviewing revisions using this system, you actually have to make three decisions for every revision you encounter:

1. How is the text marked—as a deletion or an insertion?
2. Do you want to keep the marked text or get rid of it?
3. So do you accept the revision or reject it?

Really, all you should have to think about is number 2: Do you want to keep the marked text or get rid of it? Then Word should be smart enough to deal with your decision in the appropriate way. Unfortunately, that is not the case. But if you've activated the custom keyboard shortcuts for Editor's ToolKit Plus, the following shortcuts fix the problem:

*   ALT CTRL SHIFT RIGHT ARROW takes you to the *next* revision.
*   ALT CTRL SHIFT LEFT ARROW takes you to the *previous* revision.
*   ALT CTRL SHIFT UP ARROW *retains* the current revision.
*   ALT CTRL SHIFT DOWN ARROW *removes* the current revision.

And it does so whether the revision is an insertion or a deletion, making those four keyboard shortcuts a very nice combination. You can use them to:

*   Find the next or previous revision (either insertion or deletion).
*   Retain or remove the revision (as opposed to accepting or rejecting it).

This makes reviewing revisions easy, quick, and intuitive. After you've tried it, you'll wonder how you ever managed to review revisions the old way (which, of course, you can continue to do if you like).

Formatting

Formatting

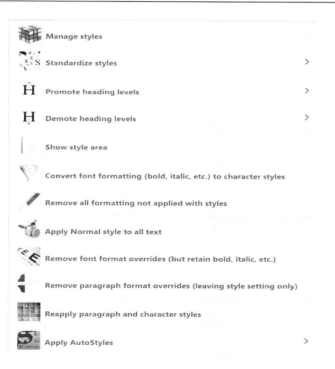

Manage styles

Standardize styles   >

Promote heading levels   >

Demote heading levels   >

Show style area

Convert font formatting (bold, italic, etc.) to character styles

Remove all formatting not applied with styles

Apply Normal style to all text

Remove font format overrides (but retain bold, italic, etc.)

Remove paragraph format overrides (leaving style setting only)

Reapply paragraph and character styles

Apply AutoStyles   >

Manage styles

This feature opens Microsoft Word's *Manage Styles* dialog without having to go through the Styles pane. Very handy!

Standardize styles

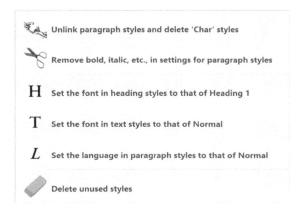

Unlink paragraph styles and delete "Char" styles

If you look carefully at Word's built-in styles, you'll notice that many of them are "linked"—a paragraph style and a character style all rolled into one. You can spot these styles by the double symbol on the right—a pilcrow followed by the letter *a:*

But a paragraph style *should* look like this, with the pilcrow alone:

And a character style should look like this, with the *a* alone:

I suspect that Microsoft created linked styles for users who (in past Word versions) selected text, tried to apply a paragraph style, and then couldn't understand why the formatting they wanted was applied to the whole paragraph rather than just their selection.

Initially, Microsoft's implementation of linked styles was done quite carelessly, with little testing (beginning in Word 97, if I recall correctly). When users selected *part* of a paragraph's text and then applied a paragraph style, Word would create and apply a new style with "Char" appended to the style name. For example, if you selected text and applied the Heading 1 style, Word would create a new style named Heading 1 Char and apply *that* rather than plain old Heading 1. What Microsoft didn't anticipate is that people would then select some text and apply the Char style, and Word would create another new style named Heading 1 Char Char. Next came Heading 1 Char Char Char, and so on. (Once you've started dancing the Char-Char, it's hard to stop.)

You've probably noticed this not-so-helpful "feature" in various documents, and it's notoriously difficult to clean up. Microsoft has fixed the problem in more recent versions of Word. However, even in Word 2019, if you apply a linked style (say Heading 1) to just *part* of a paragraph, and if the Word document is imported into

InDesign, you'll get a *character* style named Heading 1 Char in InDesign. So now your designer or typesetter is wondering what to do with that. It's not clean. It's not clear. It's not professional.

I like my paragraph styles to be paragraph styles and my character styles to be character styles, and never the twain shall meet. If you'd simply like to make paragraph styles act the way they should, go to the bottom of Word's Styles pane and check the box labeled *Disable Linked Styles.* Then applying a linked style will affect the whole paragraph, not just selected text.

But if you want to actually *unlink* styles (which I recommend), this feature will do it for you, quickly and easily. It also deletes Char styles *if* they are not applied to text in your document; otherwise, it leaves them alone. Finally, it sets base style to "(no style)" and automatic updating to false. There are two ways to access this feature:

- Formatting > Unlink paragraph styles and delete Char styles
- FileCleaner > FileCleaner Batch cleanup > Formatting tab

After the styles are unlinked, paragraph styles will affect a whole paragraph; character styles will affect only the selected text. And if your designer or typesetter imports your document into InDesign, paragraph styles will show up as paragraph styles while character styles will show up as character styles and can be formatted as needed.

Remove bold, italic, etc., in settings for paragraph styles

Paragraph styles used in editing should *not* be formatted with bold, italic, or other character formatting, as these are the editor's prerogative for marking emphasis, book titles, and so on. Even a short heading styled as Heading 1 may have one or more words marked with italic. For that reason, paragraph styles should not be set to use italic. But if your document already has paragraph styles that include character formatting, this feature will remove that formatting. Then if you italicize a word for emphasis, your intention will be clear, not muddied by the formatting of the paragraph style.

Set the font in heading styles to that of Heading 1

Let's say you're working on a manuscript in which the Heading 1 style has been set with Garamond, Heading 2 with Baskerville, and Heading 3 with Helvetica. Wouldn't it be nice if you could instantly make all those heading styles consistent? Now you can. This feature will set the font used in *all* heading styles to whatever font is used in Heading 1. Don't like the font used in Heading 1? Change the font to something else and then use this feature.

Set the font in text styles to that of Normal

Let's say you're working on a manuscript in which Normal style has been set with Garamond, Block Quote with Baskerville, and Footnote with Helvetica. Wouldn't it be nice if you could instantly make all those text styles consistent? Now you can. This feature will set the font used in *all* text styles to whatever font is used in Normal. Don't like the font used in Normal? Change the font to something else and then use this feature.

Set the language in paragraph styles to that of Normal

Let's say you're working on a manuscript in which the language in Normal style has been set to English, Block Quote has mistakenly been set to French, and Footnote text has mistakenly been set to German. Wouldn't it be nice if you could instantly make the language of all those text styles consistent? Now you can. This feature will set the language used in all paragraph styles to whatever language is used in Normal. However, it will leave the language of *character* styles untouched, making it possible to apply, say, a French character style to French words so that Spell Check will work correctly for all the text in your document. Don't like the language used in Normal? Change the language to something else and then use this feature.

Delete unused styles

Styles seem to proliferate in Microsoft Word. Built-in styles can't be deleted, but user-created styles *can* be deleted, and if your document has a bunch of them that aren't being used, why not get them out of the way? This feature will do that for you.

Promote heading levels

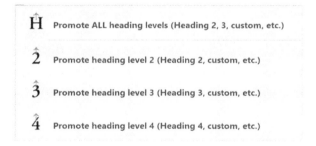

H   Promote ALL heading levels (Heading 2, 3, custom, etc.)

2   Promote heading level 2 (Heading 2, custom, etc.)

3   Promote heading level 3 (Heading 3, custom, etc.)

4   Promote heading level 4 (Heading 4, custom, etc.)

Let's say you're editing along and have marked heading levels with paragraph styles, either Word's built-in styles (such as Heading 1) or your own custom styles. Suddenly, you realize that text styled with Heading 2 should really be styled with Heading 1, that text styled with Heading 3 should be styled with Heading 2, and so on. You could tediously use Word's find and replace to take care of the problem, one style at a time, or you could use this feature to promote all heading levels at once.

- Promote ALL heading levels (Heading 2, 3, custom, etc.).

The program also allows you to individually promote some of the most commonly used headings:

- Promote heading level 2 (Heading 2, custom, etc.) to heading level 1.
- Promote heading level 3 (Heading 3, custom, etc.) to heading level 2.
- Promote heading level 4 (Heading 4, custom, etc.) to heading level 3.

Promoting *custom* heading styles won't substitute one style for another, but it will promote the outline level of the styles to the next level up.

Demote heading levels

H Demote ALL heading levels (Heading 1, 2, custom, etc.)

1 Demote heading level 1 (Heading 1, custom, etc.)

2 Demote heading level 2 (Heading 2, custom, etc.)

3 Demote heading level 3 (Heading 3, custom, etc.)

Let's say you're editing along and have marked heading levels with paragraph styles, either Word's built-in styles (such as Heading 1) or your own custom styles. Suddenly, you realize that text styled with Heading 1 should really be styled with Heading 2, that text styled with Heading 2 should be styled with Heading 3, and so on. You could tediously use Word's find and replace to take care of the problem, one style at a time, or you could use this feature to demote all heading levels at once.

- Demote ALL heading levels (Heading 1, 2, custom, etc.).

The program also allows you to individually demote some of the most commonly used headings:

- Demote heading level 1 (Heading 1, custom, etc.) to heading level 2.
- Demote heading level 2 (Heading 2, custom, etc.) to heading level 3.
- Demote heading level 3 (Heading 3, custom, etc.) to heading level 4.

Demoting *custom* heading styles won't substitute one style for another, but it will demote the outline level of the styles to the next level down.

Show styles area

If you click the *Formatting* icon and then the *Show Styles Area* icon, you'll see the Styles Area on the left of your document. The Styles Area makes it easy to see which style is applied to every paragraph in your document.

Convert font formatting (bold, italic, etc.) to character styles

If your document is going into InDesign, the paragraph styles you've applied to mark text levels will come across just fine, and your designer can then set those styles to whatever formatting is needed. Character styles will also come across just fine. Unfortunately, directly applied font formatting, such as italic, will *not* come across just fine. In fact, with InDesign's default settings, it will be lost completely. Designers can work around this problem, but only with extra work or special plugins. Why not give your designer a document with character styles already in place? This feature makes that possible for the following formatting: **bold**, *italic*, underline, double underline, superscript, subscript, ALL CAPS, SMALL CAPS, ~~strikethrough~~, ~~double strikethrough~~, and any combination thereof.

When the document is opened in InDesign, there may still be overrides on paragraph styles, but they can be removed globally in InDesign by selecting all (CMD/CTRL A) and then clicking the *Clear Overrides* button (or choosing *Clear Overrides* from the *Paragraph Style* palette flyout menu). Both the character styles *and* their formatting will remain intact.

In addition to formatting, if you've set the language of a word to "No Proofing" to prevent automatic hyphenation, this feature applies a "No Break" character style, which will also be preserved in InDesign.

This feature ignores formatting in comments, headers, and footers. It does, however, work in the main text, footnotes, endnotes, and text boxes.

If you'd like to apply character styles by default when formatting text with keyboard shortcuts, click the *Editor's ToolKit Plus* icon and then click *Set character style keyboard shortcuts.*

Remove all formatting not applied with styles

After you've used the previous feature to convert font formatting to character styles, and assuming you've used paragraph styles to mark text levels, you can use this feature to remove any formatting that is *not* applied with styles, leaving your document squeaky clean and ready for typesetting. You may still need to remove overrides in InDesign.

Apply Normal style to all text

This option applies the Normal style to the entire document, wiping out any other paragraph styles. *Warning:* If an author has used styles properly to mark various text levels, you may not want to use this option. Also, if you have used styles to format a document and want to retain them, *do not use this option.*

Remove font format overrides (but retain bold, italic, etc.)

Authors often go to great lengths to format their documents using various fonts, point sizes, and so on. What they don't realize is that such formatting, nice as it may look to them, is nowhere near the look you or your designer will specify. In fact, their formatting usually just gets in the way, making editing and typesetting more difficult than it should be.

This feature removes all directly applied font formatting, such as Times New Roman 12 point. However, it *retains* certain character formatting (bold, italic, underline, word underline, superscript, subscript, small caps, all caps, strikethrough, and hidden) as well as paragraph styles (such as Normal and Heading 1) and character styles. This leaves you with a document in which you can modify the styles to format the document properly, and in which you can convert directly applied font formatting (bold, italic, and so on) into character styles as described above.

Remove paragraph format overrides (leaving style setting only)

This option removes all directly applied paragraph formatting, such as Centered or Justified, so that paragraph formatting is handled by styles.

Reapply paragraph and character styles

Sometimes formatting just goes wonky in Word, for no apparent reason. If you reapply the paragraph style, the problem may go away. But if you're working on a big document with dozens of paragraph styles, you won't want to reapply the styles manually. This feature will do it for you.

In addition, if you're working with a document that uses multiple languages, reapplying both paragraph styles and character styles may be necessary to make language settings work as they should. For example, if you apply a French character style to some text in a paragraph but then inadvertently apply English to the whole paragraph, the French character style no longer has any effect, *even if you reapply the French character style.*

However, if you first reapply the paragraph style and *then* reapply the French character style, the language of the character style will take effect. So if you're using character styles to indicate words in a certain language but the styles don't seem to be working, now you know why. This feature will fix the problem automatically. FileCleaner allows you to reapply paragraph and character styles separately.

Marking type specs with styles

When editing on paper, you probably mark type specs by writing A, B, or C next to headings, writing "Block" next to block quotations, and so on. You can do the same thing in an electronic manuscript by using styles. For example, you can mark a main heading level by applying the style Heading 1.

Editor's ToolKit provides an easy way to apply Word's heading styles:

- To apply Heading 1, press CTRL SHIFT 1.
- To apply Heading 2, press CTRL SHIFT 2.
- And so on, through Heading 9.
- To apply the Normal style (Word's default), press CTRL SHIFT N.

Of course, styles do more than just mark levels of type. They also apply formatting to those levels. Heading 1, for example, might format a heading with 24-point Arial. I've heard people ask, "Why not just mark each heading as 24-point Arial? Why bother with styles?" If this is a question you might ask, you're about to increase your productivity. The beauty of styles is that (1) they *ensure* that formatting is consistent, and (2) they allow you to *change your mind.* Let's say you've manually formatted all of your main headings—102 of them, to be exact—as 18-point Arial, but your client thinks they should be bigger—24 points instead of 18. You now have the painful task of reformatting every one of those 102 headings[1]—unless, of course, you've used styles, in which case you can change the heading style with a few clicks of the mouse, *automatically* changing all 102 headings. Using styles provides other advantages, too:

---

[1] Okay, yes, you could also do it *en masse* with Find and Replace—*if* the headings have been consistently formatted. If they've been formatted with styles, there's no question.

- You can easily find one style and replace it with another. This is much simpler than having to search for directly applied formatting, such as 24-point Arial bold italic left justified no indent condensed by 1 point.
- If you've used Word's built-in heading styles (Heading 1 through Heading 9), you can see and change the structure of your document in Word's Outline view or Navigation pane. These headings can be applied from the Styles pane but also from the keyboard by holding down CTRL SHIFT and pressing one of the number keys (1 through 9). CTRL SHIFT N applies the Normal style. I generally use Heading 1 for part titles, Heading 2 for chapter titles, and Heading 3 for subheads in a chapter.
- Styles can be retained when importing a document into QuarkXPress or InDesign, picking up the formatting specified for those styles in the typesetter's style sheets. This also makes it possible to quickly and easily change formatting globally just by changing the style sheets. If you're a designer or typesetter and you're not using style sheets, you're spending a lot more time on formatting than you need to, and you're missing much of the power of QuarkXPress and InDesign.
- Editing is just plain *easier* after text levels have been marked up with styles, allowing you to see the *structure* of document you're working on.

The Typespec template

Included with Editor's ToolKit is a template containing various styles with which you can mark spec levels in a manuscript. The name of the template is *Typespec.dotx,* and it resides in Word's Templates folder.

Whenever you prepare a document for editing in Editor's ToolKit, the *Typespec* template is applied to it, if you so command. If you decided you didn't want it applied but later change your mind, you can make the template available to the document you're working on by following this procedure:

1. Click File > New > Personal.
2. Click Typespec.
3. Click OK.

All of the styles in the *Typespec* template should now be available. You can access the styles in the *Typespec* template using the Styles Pane or by pressing the F5 key (very handy!).

If you're going to style a single paragraph, just put your cursor anywhere in the paragraph, then select the style from the list in the window. If you're going to style more than one paragraph, first select the paragraphs you want to mark, then select the style.

The *Typespec* template uses mainly the Verdana typeface, which was created especially for viewing on-screen. Verdana lends itself well to editing because of its legibility and because its quotation marks and dashes are easily distinguishable. Another typeface that works well for editing is Georgia, which, unlike Verdana, has serifs.

You may wonder why none of the styles in the *Typespec* template uses bold or italic formatting. The reason is that using character formatting, such as bold and italic, is the editor's prerogative for marking emphasis or titles in text. Even a short heading marked with Heading 1 may have one or more individual words marked with italic for emphasis. For that reason, I've left the use of bold and italic up to you rather than trying to impose it upon you.

Please note that you can change the formatting of the *Typespec* styles any way you like. Also, you don't *have* to use the *Typespec* template for Editor's ToolKit to work. Feel free to use any document templates you like.

Special styles

Most of the styles in the *Typespec* template are easy to understand, but a few require special comment. Some of the styles end in "NI," which stands for "no indent." Use these to mark text that should have no paragraph indent. For example, use Block Quote Start NI to mark the first paragraph of a block quotation that begins somewhere in the middle of the paragraph you are quoting. Use Normal NI after a block quotation to mark text that does not begin a new paragraph but continues the thought of the text before the block quotation. Using these styles is the equivalent of writing "No paragraph" or "No indent" on a paper manuscript.

After you have marked a paragraph with one of the "NI" styles, you'll need to be sure the following paragraph is marked with a different style, or it, too, will have no indent. For example, if you're marking a block quotation that contains two paragraphs, you might mark the first paragraph with Block Quote Start NI and the following paragraph with Block End (which does include a paragraph indent). Here's an example:

Needing advice on how to handle the indenting of a block quotation, Jill found these guidelines in *The Chicago Manual of Style,* sections 10.20 and 10.25:

> If the quotation includes the beginning of the opening paragraph, it should start with a paragraph indention. If the first part of the paragraph is omitted, the opening line ordinarily begins flush left (not indented). . . .
> If, following an extract or block quotation, . . . the resuming text is a continuation of the paragraph that introduces the quotation, the resuming text should begin flush left. If the resuming text is a new paragraph, it should be given regular paragraph indention.

Jill decided to follow this advice as she began editing the massive tome.

In this example, the first paragraph is marked with Normal. The second paragraph (the first paragraph in the block quotation) is marked with Block First NI. The third paragraph (last in the block quotation) is marked with Block Last. The final paragraph is marked with Normal NI.

The reason for using the First and Last styles is so that the leading above, between, and after the paragraphs comes out right. In addition, if the block quotation above had contained four paragraphs, the second and third would have been marked with Block Middle.

I hate to mention what you have to do to mark poetry, but I will, in this little two-stanza "poem" made up of style names:

> Poem First NI
>   Poem Middle
> Poem Middle NI
>   Poem Middle
> Poem Middle NI
>   Poem End
>
> Poem Start NI
>   Poem Middle
> Poem Middle NI
>   Poem Middle
> Poem Middle NI
>   Poem Last

Marking the poem in this way allows you to use different leading before the poem, between stanzas, and after the poem, and it also allows you to adjust the indentation of each line, or even to use no indentation. Applying all those styles seems like a lot of work, but if you were editing the poem on paper, you'd basically have to do the same thing by marking line indents, extra leading, and so on.

Apply AutoStyles™

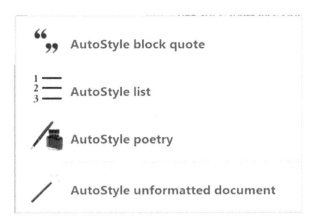

AutoStyle block quote

AutoStyle list

AutoStyle poetry

AutoStyle unformatted document

All of this marking has to be done by somebody at some point and in some way.[2] "Too much work," you say? That's why I've included the AutoStyler™ feature with Editor's ToolKit. AutoStyler makes it possible to select, say, a block quotation and instantly style it as it should be, with the first, middle, and last paragraphs all styled differently. To use this feature:

----

[2] In more recent versions of InDesign, that's no longer true for block quotations or lists, as InDesign can now suppress extra leading between paragraphs that have the same style. Recent versions of Word also have this feature. Poetry still needs extra styling, although most editors leave that to the designer or typesetter. AutoStyler takes care of all this quickly and easily, but it's no longer as important as it used to be.

1. Select the text you want to style.
2. Click the *Formatting* icon
3. Select *AutoStyle block quote, AutoStyle list,* or *AutoStyle poetry*—or press one of these shortcut key combinations:

- CTRL SHIFT B for block quote.
- CTRL SHIFT L for list.
- CTRL SHIFT P for poem.

When you're using the Poem AutoStyler, your poem can have carriage returns separating the stanzas. The Poem AutoStyler will take the carriage returns (stanza breaks) into account, style the preceding lines with the style Poem End, and delete the carriage returns.

If you're a typesetter who has been marking such styles manually, AutoStyler will make you smile.

For the AutoStyler functions to run, the following styles (used in the *Typespec* template) must exist in the active template. If they don't, AutoStyler will create them:

- Block (designates a single-paragraph block quotation)
- Block First (designates the first paragraph of a multiple-paragraph block quotation)
- Block Middle (designates any middle paragraph of a multiple-paragraph block quotation)
- Block Last (designates the last paragraph of a multiple-paragraph block quotation)

- List (designates a single-paragraph list, if there is such a thing)
- List First (designates the first item in a multiple-paragraph list)
- List Middle (designates any middle item in a multiple-paragraph list)
- List Last (designates the last item in a multiple-paragraph list)

- Poem (designates a single-line poem, if there is such a thing)
- Poem First NI (designates the first line of a poem, not indented)
- Poem Middle (designates a middle line of a stanza)
- Poem Middle NI (designates a middle line of a stanza, not indented)
- Poem Start NI (designates a line that begins a stanza, not indented)
- Poem End (designates a line that ends a stanza)
- Poem End NI (designates a line that ends a stanza, not indented)
- Poem Last (designates the last line of a poem)
- Poem Last NI (designates the last line of a poem, not indented)

AutoStyle unformatted document

Editors routinely use paragraph styles to indicate text levels in a document—headings, block quotations, and so on. But if you're working on a document that has never been styled, you may be able to get a head start by using this feature, which will style part, chapter, and section numbers; the part, chapter, and section *titles* beneath them; subheadings; and any text that appears to be a block quotation. This feature isn't perfect, but it tries really hard to do a good job, based on punctuation, indentation, paragraph alignment, and existing formatting. If your document is already styled, you shouldn't use this feature, but if it's not, you may find this feature handy, although you'll probably need to adjust some of the styling after it's done.

Navigation

Go to

Go back

Mark editing place

Find editing place

Add bookmark

H Bookmark all headings

Cockpit

Go to (all kinds of stuff)

This simply opens Word's standard Go To dialog, which you can also access with CTRL G or SHIFT F9.

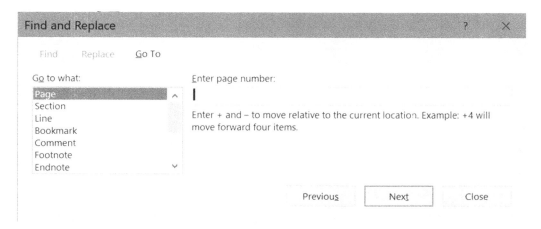

Go back (to previous edit)

"Go back" is a hard-to-find Word feature that I've made easily accessible. It takes you back to the last place you changed your document. Then the place before that. Then the place before that. In all, it cycles through the last three places you made a change. To use the feature:

- SHIFT F10
- Navigation > Go back

Mark and find editing place

Press SHIFT F11 to mark the place you were editing. Move around the document to your heart's content. Press SHIFT F12 to move back instantly to the place you marked.

Add bookmark

Microsoft Word is picky about the characters you can use in naming a bookmark. For example, you can't include a space, an ampersand, or an exclamation mark. *Add bookmark* uses the currently selected text to create a properly named bookmark and add it to the text. If no text is selected, it uses the first few words of the current paragraph.

You can also add a bookmark by pressing the CTRL key along with a number key (0-9). For example, pressing CTRL 7 adds a bookmark named "Bookmark7" to selected text or the text at your cursor position. To go *back* to that particular bookmark, press ALT CTRL plus the number key (0-9). That gives you ten bookmarks to keep track of places in your document.

Bookmark all headings

Bookmark all headings bookmarks all of the headings in your document (any text styled as Heading 1, Heading 2, and so on), automatically using the heading text as the basis for the bookmark name—handy for navigating a document, adding hyperlinks, or referencing index entries.

Many thanks to Wordmeister Steve Hudson for providing the technology behind this and the previous feature.

Cockpit

The Cockpit helps you navigate and style the documents you edit in Word. To use it, click the *Navigation* icon and then the *Cockpit* icon. Once activated, the Cockpit will *stay* activated until you deactivate it, even between Word sessions, for any document saved with the Cockpit turned on (but not for Word in general). The Cockpit icon is a toggle—click it once and the Cockpit turns on; click it again and the Cockpit turns off. You can also toggle the Cockpit with CTRL SHIFT F12.

Navigation pane

With the Cockpit activated, you'll see Word's Navigation pane on the left (unless you've moved it). If you've used Word's Heading styles (Heading 1, Heading 2, and so on) or your own custom heading styles, your headings will appear in the Navigation pane. To go to one of the headings, click the heading in the Navigation pane.

Style Inspector

Next to the Navigation pane (unless you've moved it) is the Style Inspector—very handy for seeing what style is applied to the currently selected text, identifying the formatting used in that style, modifying the style, and so on.

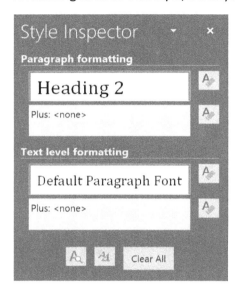

Styles area

If you click the *Formatting* icon and then the *Show Styles Area* icon, you'll see the Styles Area on the left of your document. The Styles Area makes it easy to see which style is applied to every paragraph in your document.

Heading 4

Body Text

Body Text

Heading 4

Body Text

Styles pane

On the far right of your screen (unless you've moved it), you'll see Word's Styles pane, which makes it easy to apply, modify, and manage styles. Please see Word's documentation for more information.

Special movement and deletion keys

Editor's ToolKit provides movement and deletion keys that Microsoft should have provided but didn't. It lets you:

- Move to the end of the next word: ALT RIGHT ARROW.
- Move to the end of the previous word: ALT LEFT ARROW.
- Move to the next sentence: ALT CTRL RIGHT ARROW.
- Move to the previous sentence: ALT CTRL LEFT ARROW.
- Delete to the end of the line: ALT CTRL END.
- Delete to the beginning of the line: ALT CTRL HOME.

• Delete a whole word no matter where your cursor is in the word (you won't believe what a time-saver this is): CTRL DELETE. If you press CTRL DELETE in ordinary Microsoft Word, you'll delete not the whole word but only the portion of the word to the right of the cursor. That means to delete a whole word, you have to move your cursor to the beginning of a word (unless it's already there), which is a nuisance. With Editor's ToolKit, you can place your cursor *anywhere* in a word and delete the word by pressing CTRL DELETE. I predict that you will love this feature. If you need to delete only part of a word, ALT DELETE will delete to the right of the cursor, ALT BACKSPACE to the left of the cursor.

PAGE UP and PAGE DOWN

Ordinarily in Word, when you press PAGE UP or PAGE DOWN, you'll move one screen up or down but your cursor will stay in the *same place* on your monitor. For example, if you've just finished editing a screenful of text and you move down to the next screen, the cursor will still be at the bottom of the screen. But if you've activated the custom keyboard shortcuts in Editor's ToolKit Plus, your cursor will go to the top of the *page,* where it belongs (in Draft view, only if Zoom is set at 100% or less). This makes a real difference in the "feel" of editing on the computer, especially if you have a big monitor or one that can be pivoted to portrait rather than landscape orientation.

If for some strange reason you actually *want* your cursor to stay at the same position while moving up or down a screen, press ALT PAGE UP or ALT PAGE DOWN.

If you want to move to the top or bottom of the current *screen,* ALT CTRL PAGE UP or ALT CTRL PAGE DOWN will do the job.

To move to the previous or the next paragraph (very handy), press CTRL UP or CTRL DOWN.

Document

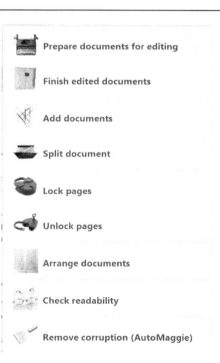

Prepare documents for editing

Finish edited documents

Add documents

Split document

Lock pages

Unlock pages

Arrange documents

Check readability

Remove corruption (AutoMaggie)

Prepare documents for editing

Before you work on documents using Editor's ToolKit, there are certain things you'll probably want to do to them. These include applying a template, locking pages, turning on revision marking, and other options. Click *Document > Prepare Documents for editing.* Then choose the options you'd like to use in preparing your documents:

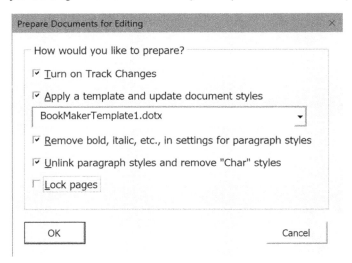

Use the dropdown list to select a template to apply to your documents. The Typespec.dotx template included with Editor's ToolKit Plus is a good choice for editing.

After you click OK, the program will ask if you want to prepare the active document, all open documents, or all documents in a folder. Choose the option that meets your needs.

Finish edited documents

Finish edited documents performs the following operations:

- Turn off track changes
- Make revisions permanent
- Remove highlighting
- Delete comments
- Unlock pages
- Remove metadata, including personal information (your name in comments, for example) along with document information and properties, so you can keep your private information private.

Prepare documents for InDesign or other layout program

In addition, Finish Edited Documents includes options that prepare your documents for import into InDesign or other layout programs. These include:

- Unlink paragraph styles and remove "Char" styles.
- Delete unused styles.
- Remove bold, italic, etc., in settings for paragraph styles.
- Convert font formatting (bold, italic, etc.) to character styles (*essential* for documents used in a layout program).
- Remove all formatting (overrides) not applied with styles.

When you click the OK button, the program will ask if you want to prepare the active document, all open documents, or all documents in a folder. Choose the option that meets your needs.

Add documents

Often when I go to edit a book, I discover that the author's chapters have been saved as individual documents. I usually put all of these together in one long document, which makes it easier to make things consistent, find and replace items throughout the book, and so on. The "Add Documents" program makes it easy to bring a whole folder full of documents into a single document for editing.

To use the program, you must first make sure your documents are named alphabetically in the order in which they should appear, since that is the order in which the program will add them to your document. For example, you might name them something like this:

> Chapter 01
> Chapter 02
> Chapter 03
> . . .
> Chapter 10
> Chapter 11

And so on.

If you name them like this, you'll have problems:

> Chapter 1
> Chapter 2
> Chapter 3
> . . .
> Chapter 10

The documents will be combined in the wrong order, because your computer will see them in alphabetical order, like this:

> Chapter 1
> Chapter 10
> Chapter 2
> Chapter 3

If you open the folder in which the documents reside and list them alphabetically, they should appear in the order you want them. If they don't, you'll need to rename them so they do. Also, make sure no other documents are in the folder. If other files are there, they, too, will be added to the long document. Show all types of files to be sure.

When you're ready to combine the documents, follow this procedure:

1. Create a new document on your screen or open an existing document to which you want to add the others.
2. Click *Document > Add files.*
3. Select the folder in which your documents reside.

The documents will be added, in order, to the active document, separated by section breaks.

Split document

After I've edited a long document, such as a book, I sometimes split it up into smaller files by chapter, since I know that many typesetters prefer working with smaller files in QuarkXPress or InDesign. The "Split document" feature makes this easy to do.

You can split a document at various points:

*   Manual page breaks.
*   Section breaks.
*   Paragraphs styled with Heading 1.
*   Paragraphs styled with any Heading level (1-9).

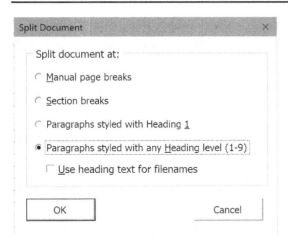

If you want to split at manual page breaks or section breaks, your document will need to include a manual page break or section break at every point you want your document to be split. Do not, however, insert a break at the top or bottom of your document.

Once you've selected the option you want to use, click the OK button. The program will copy each part into a new document and save that document, using a name that begins with the first four characters of the original document name followed by four digits, starting with 0001. For example, if your original document is named CHAPTERS, the split-off documents will have names like this:

CHAP0001
CHAP0002
CHAP0003

If you select either of the last two options (Paragraphs styled with Heading 1 or Paragraphs styled with any heading level), you can opt to use the heading text for the filenames of the separate documents. In either case, the new documents will be saved in the same folder that holds your original document.

Lock pages

One problem editors have working on a computer is that they lose their sense of proportion about the manuscript. What do I mean by sense of proportion? While working on a paper manuscript, with the pages piled neatly on the desktop, editors know exactly how much work they've done: 112 pages, stacked on the left, are finished; 204 pages, stacked on the right, are left to edit. In my experience, they also know that chapter 3 is about, oh, half an inch from the bottom in the left-hand stack if they need to go back to it. And they know, semi-consciously, that the odd foreign word the author used was about twenty pages back and about a third of the way down the page. In other words, they have a "positional memory" that helps them find things. It's not as precise as Word's "find" function, but it's still very useful.

Editing on the computer throws this out of whack, because on the computer there are no discrete pages, just one long, solid mass of text that scrolls up and down. I know which "page" I'm on because Microsoft Word tells me the number ("Page 17 of 84") on its status bar. Still, when I fixed that misspelling, it was about half an inch from the top of the screen, but where is it now? And on what page? Who knows?

A fairly workable solution consists of "locking" the pages, using column breaks to separate that long string of text into discrete pages, and setting the page length to its maximum of 22 inches. Then if you add text on a page, the text won't reflow over other pages (unless you've added more than 11 inches of text), which helps solve the positional-memory problem.

With locked pages, Editor's ToolKit plays fast and loose with such things as page size because it assumes that at this point in the publishing process you don't really care about such things as page size or even point size because you are editing, not typesetting. (Locked pages work best in Draft view.) Typesetting comes later in the publishing process. If you're trying to do typesetting, copy fitting, or final formatting with Microsoft Word, you probably don't want to lock or unlock pages.

Caution: If you've locked your pages, remember that they're now 22 inches long, which means you probably don't want to print them in that condition. Before printing, unlock your pages to return them to their original size.

Unlock pages

Unlocking pages, as you might think, undoes what happens when you lock pages. It removes column breaks and sets page height to its original size.

Arrange documents

When comparing two documents, editors usually put the reference document on the left and the working document on the right. Word includes a feature that does that, but it's not easy to find. It's on the *View* tab under *Window > View Side by Side.*

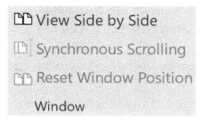

When you activate the feature, *Synchronous Scrolling,* which is just underneath it, turns on automatically. That may sometimes be useful, but I usually turn it off—another small annoyance.

Editor's ToolKit Plus provides an editor's version of *View Side by Side* called *Arrange documents.* This feature offers some advantages over the standard Word version (which you can continue to use, of course):

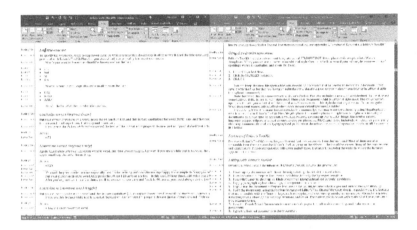

- It automatically turns *off* synchronous scrolling.
- To conserve screen space, it turns off currently open task panes (such as the Navigation pane and the Styles pane). This allows you to focus on the documents themselves without having to turn off all those panes manually, which is a bit of a nuisance in Word's native version.
- It automatically restores previously displayed task panes when the documents are "unarranged."
- It's a toggle! If the documents are not already arranged, it arranges them; if they *are* already arranged, it *unarranges* them.

- It displays your documents side by side using the view setting of the first document you opened. For example, if you set the view for that document as Draft view, *both* documents will be displayed in Draft view.

Movement and views

Arrange documents displays the first document you opened on the left, the second document you opened on the right. You can go back and forth between the two documents with your mouse, with ALT TAB, or with CTRL SHIFT F6. If you change the view in one document (for example, from Draft to Print), *both* documents will change views for easy comparison.

Viewing a single document in two windows

Arrange documents won't work with more than two open documents, but it *will* work with just *one* open document, automatically duplicating the display of that document in a new window and then arranging the two windows side by side. This is a convenient way to compare different parts of a document. For example, you might have the main text on the left and the bibliography on the right so you can check bibliography entries against source citations in the text. You can scroll through the windows independently. Any change you make to the text in one window will also be made in the other, which, since it's actually the same document, makes perfect sense. There are two ways to access this feature:

- CTRL SHIFT F5 (toggle)
- Document > Arrange documents (toggle)

Check readability

This feature displays various statistics about your document. To learn more, search online for information about readability and how it can be used to improve your editing. For example, if "Sentences per Paragraph," "Words per Sentence," and "Characters per Word" are all on the high side, editing to reduce those numbers will make your document easier to read, as will reducing the number of passive sentences.

The Flesch-Kincaid Grade Level score shows the educational grade level of the text. For example, a score of 8 means the text is suitable for 8th-graders. The Flesch Reading Ease score ranges from 0 to 100; the higher the score, the more readable the text. A score of 90 is approximately 5th-grade level; 70 is 7th-grade; 50 is 12th-grade.

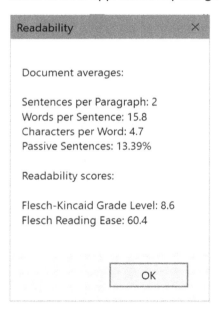

Remove corruption (AutoMaggie™)

Early word processors, such as WordPerfect, kept track of text and formatting as a clean, continuous string of characters and codes that looked like this:

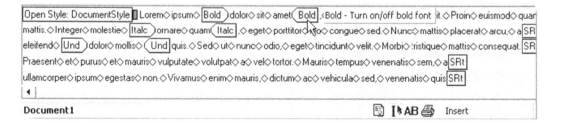

When creating Word, Microsoft took a different approach, using numeric pointers to specify what was going on in a document. For example, characters 7 through 15 of paragraph 10 might be given the attribute of italic. (That's not technically exact; I'm just trying to convey the general idea here.) A typical Word document has thousands of these pointers, which are stored in paragraph breaks and section breaks. Pointers for the document as a whole are stored in its final paragraph break. The problem is, those pointers can—and sometimes do—get out of whack and end up pointing at the wrong thing, which results in document corruption, with symptoms like these:

- Repeatedly renumbering pages.
- Repeatedly rebreaking pages.
- Incorrect layout and formatting.
- Strange or unreadable characters.
- Error messages.
- Missing text.
- Text that shouldn't be there.
- Computer lockups and crashes.

Document corruption is usually caused by one or more of the following:

* Moving documents with tracked revisions from PC to Macintosh or vice versa.
* Master documents.
* Nested tables.
* Automatic list numbering.
* Automatically updated document styles.
* Fields, especially cross-references.
* Deleted note numbers (in the notes themselves, not in the main text).
* Saving when resources are low.
* A corrupt printer driver.
* A corrupt document template, especially Normal.dotm.

The standard solution is to "maggie" the document (a process named by Wordmeister Steve Hudson for technical writer Margaret Secara from the TECHWR-L mailing list):

1. Select all of the text in the document.
2. Hold down SHIFT and press the LEFT ARROW key to deselect the final paragraph mark.
3. Copy the selected text.
4. Create a new document.
5. Paste the text into the new document.
6. Use the new document rather than the old one.

That, however, may not be enough. If your document has section breaks, they too can hold corruption, which means you'll need to maggie each section separately—selecting its text, deselecting the section break at the end, and copying and pasting the text into a new document, adding new section breaks as needed. If you have lots of sections, this will take lots of time.

Fortunately, the "Remove corruption" feature will do all of this for you. In addition, it replaces all paragraph breaks with shiny new ones, leaving your document free of corruption. Probably. We hope.

Text

 Convert tables, textboxes, and frames to color-shaded text	›
Modify existing text	›
© Insert special characters	›
LOREM IPSUM Insert generic text	
Use the Spike	›
Remove highlighting	
text Convert hyperlinks to regular text	
Create or edit editorial style sheet (ctrl shift e)	
Alphabetically sort editorial style sheet	
$\sum$ Identify next character	

Convert tables, text boxes, and frames to regular text

These features convert tables, text boxes, or frames to regular text in the active document, shading the text's background in yellow, blue, or gray so you can *see* what used to be tables, text boxes, or frames as you edit. The feature includes a utility to remove the colored shading after your review.

Modify existing text

Make word italic or roman (toggle)

This feature jumps from word to word at the touch of a key, changing italic words to roman, and roman words to italic. It's great when you're editing authors who have forgotten to italicize book titles or who have italicized the titles of magazine articles. You can also use this feature to toggle italic on selected text. To use it:

- F8
- Text > Modify existing text > Make word italic or roman

Capitalize or lowercase word (toggle)

Put your cursor anywhere on a word and this feature capitalizes (initial cap) or lowercases the word and moves your cursor to the next word. This feature also turns a word in all caps to one that's lowercase.

If you use this feature while text is selected, the text will be formatted in proper title case, just as if you'd clicked *Title-case selected text* under the *Editor's ToolKit* menu.

Title-case selected text

Select the words you'd like to be in Title-Case, then use this feature. If you use it with a title-case list (more information below), it will follow the case of the words on your list but title-case everything else. If you *don't* use a title-case list, it will title-case everything except the following common articles, conjunctions, and prepositions: *a, an, and, at, but, by, for, from, in, into, of, off, on, onto, or, out, over, the, through, to, under, unto, and with.* This feature also title-cases the first and last words in the selected text, as well as the first word after a colon or terminal punctuation. This is extremely useful if you're working on a document with headings in all caps that need to be in proper title case.

- F9 with text selected
- Text > Modify existing text > Title-case selected text

Incidentally, if you need a heading to be in all caps, LIKE THIS, you shouldn't *type* it in all caps. Rather, you should make it title case and then format it as all caps in the style used with the heading. That way, if your design changes from all caps (or goes to a typesetter), the words will be in proper-title case format with the modified style.

Title-case all text styled as Heading 1, 2, custom, etc.

If your headings are styled as headings, using Heading 1, Heading 2 (etc.), or custom heading styles you've created, this feature will automatically and *properly* (based on your title-case list or the defaults listed above) title-case all headings in the active document, all open documents, or all documents in a folder. It can also be run as an option in FileCleaner.

Edit title-case list

To specify the words you *don't* want to be title-cased, you'll need the title-case list (*TitleCaseList.docx*). This list must be kept in your default Documents folder, where Editor's ToolKit Plus expects to find it. A partial list is provided with Editor's ToolKit Plus, but you should modify it to meet your needs. To edit the list, click *Text > Edit title-case list*.

- If the list includes words in lowercase (such as *of, to, a, but,* and *the*), those words will be set in lowercase in your headings unless the words follow a colon or terminal punctuation.
- If the list includes words in UPPERCASE (such as *USA, NATO,* and *AARP*), those words will be set in UPPERCASE in your headings.
- If the list includes words in MixedCase (such as *FileCleaner* and *DEXembed*), those words will be set in MixedCase in your headings.

If the list is not available, commonly used articles, conjunctions, and prepositions will be used instead: *a, an, and, at, but, by, for, from, in, into, of, off, on, onto, or, out, over, the, through, to, under, unto,* and *with.*

Capitalize a word (keyboard only)

Put your cursor anywhere on a word, press the F9 function key, and this feature capitalizes the word (initial cap) and then moves your cursor to the next word. That means you can jump from word to word, capping as you go. This feature also turns a word in all caps to one that's cap and lowercase.

Note: If you press the F9 key *while text is selected,* the text will be formatted in proper title case, just as if you'd clicked *Text > Title-case selected text.* You'll find this a handy way to title-case a selection.

Lowercase a word (keyboard only)

Again, this feature lets you jump from word to word, this time lowercasing all the way. If you use it while text is selected, the text will be formatted in lower case. This is handy if you have several words in a row that need to be made lower case so you can apply small-cap character formatting. To use it, press the F10 function key.

This and the previous feature are especially useful when editing authors who are cap-happy. For example, let's say you're editing a manuscript in which the author has capitalized chapter headings like this: "CHAPTER ONE: THE GHOST IN THE MACHINE."

Put your cursor on the first word, then press the F9 and F10 keys as needed—in this case, F9 four times, F10 twice, and F9 once again. Here's the result: "Chapter One: The Ghost in the Machine."

After you've practiced this a few times, you'll be amazed at how easy and fast it is. Of course, you could always do the job with *Make selection title case,* as explained above, but alternately using the F9 and F10 keys gives you more immediate control.

Transpose words

Don't you wish Word had a way to transpose words? Now it does. For example, you can turn "said she" to "she said" at the touch of a key. Place your cursor anywhere on the *second* of the two words you want to transpose. Then press F11.

Transpose characters

One keystroke turns "rihgt" into "right." Place your cursor between the two characters you want to transpose. Then press F12.

Extend selection (keyboard only)

Extend Selection is a terrific Word feature you may not know about. I've made it accessible on what at first seems a strange place: the INSERT key. I don't like having the Insert key turn on typeover mode, which should always be turned off while editing and usually at all other times. Word also allows you to use the INSERT key to paste text (see the *Options* menu), but I've found it too easy to hit the key accidentally and paste unwanted text into a document without even knowing it. Thus, I've opted to use the INSERT key for *Extend Selection,* and you'll find that's a handy key on which to have it.

Basically, *Extend Selection* turns on the selecting of text. Then you can use the cursor keys to move through the text, selecting as you go. The really neat thing for editing is that you can put your cursor at the beginning of the text you want to select, then activate *Extend Selection,* then type the character that's at the *end* of the text you want to select. The selection will automatically jump to that character. I use this feature a lot to select to the period at the end of a sentence and to select to a carriage return at the end of a paragraph (in order to delete the selected text). If you press the INSERT key twice, you'll select the current word; three times, the current sentence; four times, the current paragraph; and five times, all the text in the document. Press the ESCAPE key to move your cursor to the end of the selection and automatically turn the selection off (a feature exclusive to Editor's ToolKit Plus).

Insert Special Characters

Insert special characters makes it easy to insert commonly used special characters into your document.

$\frac{1}{M}$ Em dash

$\frac{1}{N}$ En dash

●   Bullet

©   Copyright

TM   Trademark

®   Registered

Insert generic text

Insert generic text inserts generic text into your document. This is useful if you need junk text to experiment with or if you're setting up paragraph styles. The feature includes several options:

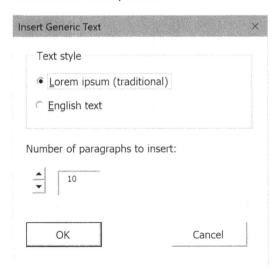

Lorem ipsum text looks like this:

> Lorem ipsum dolor sit amet, consectetur adipiscing elit, sed do eiusmod tempor incididunt ut labore et dolore magna aliqua. Ut enim ad minim veniam, quis nostrud exercitation ullamco laboris nisi ut aliquip ex ea commodo consequat.

English text looks like this:

> But I must explain to you how all this mistaken idea of denouncing pleasure and praising pain was born and I will give you a complete account of the system, and expound the actual teachings of the great explorer of the truth, the master-builder of human happiness.

Use the Spike

Cut to Spike

Copy to Spike

Insert Spike

Cut to Spike

Remember when editors wore green celluloid visors and impaled pieces of paper on a shiny steel spike? Word, too, has a spike, but it's buried so deep that most Word users have never even heard of it. I've brought it up to the surface. The spike is a *cumulative* cut and paste. It lets you cut as many blocks of text as you like and then paste them all at once in your chosen location.

Note: Word's spike feature has a bug: it pastes marked revisions as regular text, which means the text you've deleted comes back again along with the text you've added—just a mess. Editor's ToolKit overcomes this problem by making permanent any revisions in the spiked text before it is pasted. Just so you know.

- CTRL F5
- Text > Use the Spike > Cut to Spike

Copy to Spike

Sometimes, rather than *cutting* text to the spike, you'll want to *copy* text to the spike, leaving the existing text in place. When you do that, there's no way to allow for the bug described above under "Spike," so be careful.

- ALT CTRL F5 (not listed on the keyboard template)
- Text > Copy to Spike

Insert Spike

The text is pasted at your cursor position in the order in which it was cut or copied—first in, first out. If you're rearranging massive chunks of text, you'll like spike.

- CTRL F6
- Text > Use the Spike > Insert spike

Remove highlighting

This feature removes all highlighting from the active document.

Convert hyperlinks to regular text

Text copied from websites often includes hyperlinks. This feature converts them to regular text in the active document.

Create or edit editorial style sheet

This feature opens the document named EditorialStyleSheet.docx if it exists in your default Documents folder. If it doesn't exist there, the feature creates the document and opens it for your use. You can use the document to keep track of your editorial decisions for a particular project. The document doubles as a MegaReplacer master list and looks like this:

FIND	Format	REPLACE	Format	Highlight	Option	Comment
!!!!		!				
!!!		!				
!!		!				
%		percent				
&		and				
accidently		accidentally				
accomodate		accommodate				
accomodation		accommodation				
accordian		accordion				
acknowledgement		acknowledgment				
acquaintence		acquaintance				
adjacent to		next to				
albeit		though				
all of the		all the				
alot		a lot			w	
alright		all right				
amidst		amid				
amongst		among				

You can enter an incorrect usage in the "FIND" column and a corresponding correct usage in the "REPLACE" column, along with any necessary explanation in the "Comments" column (or above and below the table). You can then use the style sheet with MegaReplacer to enforce your editorial decisions in other chapters or projects.

To open the editorial style sheet, press CTRL SHIFT E. The style sheet will open with the cursor in a new row. If your cursor was on a word before you opened the style sheet, the word will be added to your clipboard, and you can paste it into the style sheet wherever you like. You can also select text you want to add before you open the style sheet. Again, the text will be added to your clipboard, ready to be pasted into the style sheet.

Alphabetically sort editorial style sheet

At some point, you may find your editorial style sheet becoming unwieldy because it includes so many entries. To make the style sheet easier to navigate, use this feature to sort its entries alphabetically.

Identify next character

Word documents often include odd characters that you need to find and replace or otherwise deal with. But that may be hard to do unless you know the character's ANSI or Unicode number. Let's say you're searching for em dashes using the standard Word code, ^+, but it doesn't work, even though you can *see* the dashes in your document. If you put your cursor in front of a dash and then use this feature, it will tell you that the "dash" has a Unicode number of 9472. Now you can search for those characters using the code ^u9472 and replace them with the standard em dash (using the ^+ code), which will be translated correctly in InDesign.

Here's the result you'd get if you placed your cursor in front of the *micro* character
(lowercase Greek *mu*) and then selected this feature:

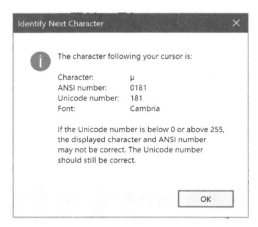

The font is also identified because some fonts have different characters for the same
ANSI number, although the Unicode number for a character should (theoretically)
never vary. (See my *Wildcard Cookbook* for more information about stuff like this:
ISBN 978-1-4341-0398-7.)

FileCleaner

Have you ever wished you could quickly and easily clean up common editorial and typographical problems in a manuscript without tediously finding and replacing each one? FileCleaner lets you do just that, replacing multiple spaces with single spaces, changing multiple returns to single returns, turning underlining to italic, fixing spacing around ellipses, and much, much more. FileCleaner will save you hours of time while improving the quality and consistency of everything you write or edit.

FileCleaner is especially useful to people who are using Microsoft Word as a "front end" for such programs as InDesign. Editors and typesetters will find it invaluable. FileCleaner is also an excellent tool for desktop or electronic publishing, and writers will appreciate being able to clean up common manuscript problems in one fell swoop.

Running FileCleaner

You can use FileCleaner to clean up documents in two different ways:

- *One item at a time.* You can do this by clicking the individual items on the *FileCleaner* menu.

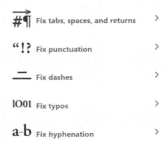

This is handy for quickly cleaning up minor problems as you come across them while editing a document. This type of cleanup affects only the part of the document you are in. For example, if you are in a footnote panel, it will clean up the footnotes. If you are in the main text, that is what will be cleaned up. *Please note:* These individual items do *not* track revisions, even if tracking is turned on in your document.

• Several selected items at once (batch cleanup). Do this by clicking the FileCleaner menu and then FileCleaner batch cleanup.

FileCleaner batch cleanup

 **FileCleaner batch cleanup** >>>

This option is useful for cleaning up multiple problems at one time, and it includes *many* more options than the individual items on the menu. It is very powerful and is probably the one you will use (and *should* use) the most.

FileCleaner's batch cleanup shows you a list of items you might want to clean up, and you can check the ones you want to use. In the 2014 version of Editor's ToolKit Plus, all of FileCleaner's batch options were displayed in one large window, like this:

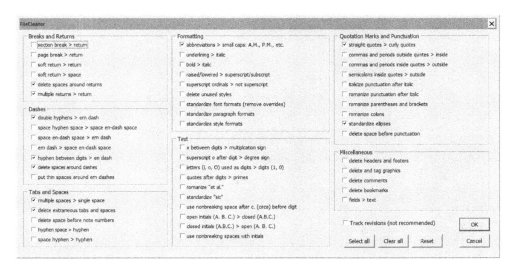

I've since added so many additional (and useful!) options that it's become necessary to put each kind of option on its own tab.

FileCleaner Batch Cleanup   ×

| Breaks, Returns, Spaces, Tabs | Dashes | Hyphenation |
| Formatting | Text | Punctuation | Miscellaneous |

☐ properly title-case heading styles (Heading 1, 2, custom, etc.)

☐ x between digits > multiplication sign
☐ superscript o after digit > degree sign
☐ letters (l, o, O) used as digits > digits (1, 0)
☐ quotes after digits > primes

☐ romanize "et al." "i.e." "e.g." "et al" "ie" "eg"
☐ italicize "et al." "i.e." "e.g." "et al" "ie" "eg"
☐ add period after "et al" if not at sentence end
☐ remove period after "et al." if not at sentence end
☐ add comma after "et al." or "et al" if not at sentence end
☐ standardize "sic"

☐ open initials (A. B. C.) > closed (A.B.C.)
☐ closed initials (A.B.C.) > open (A. B. C.)

☐ regular page ranges (123-124) > Chicago style (123-24)
☐ Chicago page ranges (123-24) > regular style (123-124)

| Select all on tab | Clear all on tab | Reset tab |

| Select all | Clear all | Reset all |

To save your options from this session, enter a name for it here:

[▼]

To select a saved session, click the drop-down arrow on the right.

To delete a saved session: Delete selected session

| OK | | Cancel |

Those tabs are:

- Breaks, Returns, Spaces, Tabs
- Dashes
- Hyphenation
- Formatting
- Text
- Punctuation
- Miscellaneous

For the most part, the options in FileCleaner's batch cleanup are self-explanatory; those that aren't are covered individually elsewhere in this documentation.

Please don't just select options willy-nilly. Review the options and select only those you need. The buttons labeled *Select all* and *Clear all* can give you a starting point, and you can refine things from there. If you click the button labeled *Reset All,* the options selected the last time FileCleaner ran will be selected again. You can use those buttons for the items on each tab or for all of the tabs together.

After you've finished selecting the items you want to clean up, click the *OK* button. FileCleaner will do the job as you requested. When it is done, it will display a message saying "Finished!" Click *OK,* then review your cleaned-up documents. If you change your mind, go back to your original, backed-up files. You did back them up, right?

FileCleaner saved settings

In previous versions, FileCleaner could remember the last options that you selected, but several people have asked for the ability to save entire *sets* of options for future use. You can do that using the input box at the bottom of FileCleaner's batch cleanup dialog:

To save your options from this session, enter a name for it here:

To select a saved session, click the drop-down arrow on the right.

Just enter a name for a set of options (for a certain client, a certain kind of manuscript, or whatever). Then click *OK* to clean up those options. The next time you use FileCleaner, you can select that set of options again by clicking the drop-down arrow on the right. When you do, all of the options for that saved setting will become selected.

You can save up to 20 different settings. If you try to save more than 20, your new setting will become the first on the list, while number 20 will be deleted to make room. All other settings will move down one position, with setting 2 becoming setting 3, setting 3 becoming setting 4, and so on.

You can also delete settings. To do so, select the setting from the dropdown list. Then click the button labeled "Delete selected session":

To delete a saved session: Delete selected session

FileCleaner options

Here are some of the most commonly used cleaning options FileCleaner provides. These are available on the dropdown menu, but many more options are available in the FileCleaner batch cleanup dialog.

Put abbreviations in small caps

This option sets A.M., P.M., B.C., A.D., B.C.E., and C.E. in small caps, which is how they should appear typographically. It also sets AM, PM, BC, AD, BCE, and CE in small caps, in case you're not using periods with abbreviations. Please note that if you abbreviate "chief executive officer" as C.E.O. (with periods) or CEO (without periods), the abbreviation will be ignored; in other words, it will *not* be set in small caps.

Change underlining to italics

This option changes text that is underlined into text that is italicized. In the days before word-processing, people used typewriter underlining to indicate text that was to be set in italics. Some writers, even though they are now composing on the computer, still continue in that tradition. Underlining, however, should not ordinarily be used in typesetting, and this option allows you to turn it into italics as it should be.

Change raised/lowered text to superscript/subscript

This option changes text that is raised into superscript, and text that is lowered into subscript, which is what is needed for typesetting.

Delete extraneous tabs

The proper way to set paragraph indentation is with formatting in a style, not with a tab. That means all tabs at the beginnings of paragraphs should be deleted; tabs at the *end* of paragraphs should also be deleted. This option does the trick. It also replaces multiple tabs inside paragraphs with single tabs so tabular formatting can be done correctly by adjusting tab settings.

Replace multiple spaces with single spaces

Your high-school typing teacher probably told you to put double spaces after the end of each sentence to make your typing "easier to read." Actually, this is a typographical abomination that must be cleaned up before a document is typeset. This option turns any combination of spaces into one space.

Delete spaces around returns

Spaces around carriage returns are invisible to the eye, but they cause various typographical problems. This option gets rid of them, even in footnotes and endnotes.

Replace multiple returns with single returns

Ordinarily, the proper way to set extra leading between paragraphs or after headings is with formatting in a style, not with extra carriage returns. Unfortunately, authors often use multiple returns to add space between paragraphs, like this.¶

¶

FileCleaner can turn any combination of returns into a single return, even in footnotes and endnotes, which is almost impossible to do by hand. If you try, you'll usually get an error message:

But FileCleaner solves the problem everywhere, including notes.

Warning: If an author has used multiple returns to indicate special formatting, you'll want to use this option with caution.

Fix spacing around ellipses

Authors have numerous ways of typing ellipses. Some use the horrid little ellipses "character" created for "desktop publishing." (The character doesn't exist in traditional typesetting.) Other authors type three periods in a row with no spacing in between. And there are many other variations. This option fixes them all, with three periods separated by spaces. The spaces after the first two ellipsis points are nonbreaking so the ellipsis points won't break at the end of a line. Perfect.

Change straight quotation marks to curly ones

This feature turns "straight"quotation marks and apostrophes as found on a typewriter ("like these") into typographically correct "curly" marks.

This feature also turns single quotation marks at the beginning of certain words into apostrophes. Those words are:

- 'tis
- 'Tis
- 'tisn't
- 'Tisn't
- 'tain't
- 'Tain't
- 'twas
- 'Twas
- 'twasn't
- 'Twasn't
- 'twere
- 'Twere
- 'tweren't
- 'Tweren't
- 'twill
- 'Twill
- 'twon't
- 'Twon't
- 'twould
- 'Twould
- 'twouldn't
- 'Twouldn't

- 'til
- 'Til
- 'cause
- 'Cause
- 'bout
- 'Bout
- 'round
- 'Round
- 'fore
- 'Fore
- 'im
- 'er
- 'em
- 'n'
- 'riting
- 'ritin'
- 'rithmetic

The same is true of single quotation marks in front of numbers, such as '99. Otherwise, this option turns apostrophes at the beginning of words into single quotation marks, which is almost always what they should be.

Fix commas and periods outside quotation marks

In American usage, commas and periods should be "inside" (to the left of) closing quotation marks. This option puts them where they belong. British users will disagree and can select the option to fix commas and periods that are *inside* quotation marks.

Fix punctuation marks outside italics

Punctuation should usually be typeset in the style of the text that precedes it. For example, if a word set in italic type is followed by a question mark, the question mark, too, should be set in italic type. This option makes it so for periods, commas, colons, semicolons, question marks, and exclamation points. British users will disagree and can select the option to fix punctuation marks that are *inside* italics.

Change double hyphens to em dashes

Many authors use double hyphens to indicate em dashes--like this. This option turns them into true dashes.

Change hyphens between numerals to en dashes

En dashes are used primarily to indicate inclusive numbers, as in an index. Many authors use hyphens to serve the same purpose, like this: 145-46. This option changes those hyphens into typographically correct en dashes.

Delete spaces around em dashes

Some authors think it looks nice to leave spaces around em dashes. If you disagree, this option removes those spaces.

Change ells used as ones to ones

Remember typewriters? They usually didn't have a character for the numeral one. The ell did double duty to keep the number of keys to a minimum. Now, decades later, some authors still type ells for ones, creating a typographic nightmare. This option fixes the problem while leaving real ells intact.

Change os used as zeroes to zeroes

This problem is similar to the previous one. Some authors type an O when they should type a zero, but typographically the two characters are not the same. This option fixes the mistake.

Repair missing note numbers in footnotes and endnotes

The superscript numbers in front of footnotes and endnotes are called note numbers (not to be confused with superscript *reference* numbers, which are up in the main text).

Footnotes | All Footnotes

[1] This is a note.

[2] This is another note.

———

What's interesting about note numbers is that it's possible to *delete* them, so that the notes look like this:

Footnotes All Footnotes

> This is a note.

> This is another note.

> ——

Deleting them, however, is an extraordinarily bad idea. Those numbers may look simple, but under the hood they have a lot going on. The number is automatically generated based on the reference number up in the text. (If you create footnote 9 in your text, the note will start with the number 9. If you delete footnote 9 in your text, the note and its number will be deleted.) The number also signals the start of a new note, and if it's gone, document corruption is probably not far behind.

You can often tell if a note number is missing by looking at the other note numbers. If they're numbered like this, you know something's wrong:

Footnotes All Footnotes

> [1] This is a note.

> This is another note.

> [3] And yet another note.

> ——

That's actually a fairly easy problem to fix: just copy the number from one of the other notes and paste it in front of the note that's missing its number. For example, if you copy the number for note 3 and paste it in front of the numberless note 2, you'll actually get a 2 in front of the note. Microsoft Word is smart enough to know what the number should be.

Usually the reason a number is missing is because the author has directly deleted the entire text of the note (except for the final carriage return, which can't be deleted), like this:

Footnotes All Footnotes

[1] This is a note.

[3] And yet another note.

———

Why Microsoft hasn't prevented this is beyond me. If the author had deleted the note number up in the main document text, there wouldn't be a problem.

Sometimes, in an effort to make notes look "pretty" or meet a certain style, authors will format reference numbers as regular text rather than superscript, then type a period after them. There's really nothing wrong with that, other than introducing extraneous periods when importing the file into a typesetting program. But some authors actually *delete* the numbers and type in new ones by hand. You can tell when that's been done by putting your cursor in front of a double-digit note number and pressing the right cursor key. If your cursor moves past the entire number, the number has been automatically generated. But if your cursor moves forward only one digit, the number has been hand-typed.

All of these problems can be fixed by hand, but it's tedious work. Instead, let FileCleaner do it for you.

Unlink headers and footers

By default, headers and footers in a Word document are linked to each other, so that if you change the text of one heading, the others follow suit, even if that's not what you wanted. Unlinking headers and footers solves the problem, putting you back in control.

Delete headers and footers

If you're editing a document destined for typesetting in InDesign or QuarkXPress, you don't need headers and footers. In fact, they can just get in the way. This feature gets rid of them.

Combine lines improperly broken with hard or soft returns

If you're editing a document that includes text pasted from a PDF,¶
each line of a paragraph may end with a carriage return, like this:¶
You can't just find and replace those returns with spaces because¶
that would also wipe out legitimate carriage returns at the ends¶
of paragraphs, like this one:¶

In some documents, you may also see lines that are broken with soft returns, which look like a little crooked arrow pointing inward.

Without FileCleaner, you'd have to fix both kinds of breaks like this:

1. Manually tag the true end of every paragraph with an arbitrary code, like this: |~|
2. Use find and replace to turn all returns into spaces (use the ^p code for hard returns, the ^l code for soft returns).
3. Use find and replace to turn all of your codes (|~|) into carriage returns (using the ^p code).

But on a long document, that's still a lot of work. Instead, use this feature in FileCleaner, which automatically fixes both kinds of improper breaks, joining lines that shouldn't be broken and retaining legitimate breaks as needed.

Note: This feature isn't magic; on rare occasions it may break a paragraph where it shouldn't be broken, so you'll need to watch for that. Overall, however, it does a surprisingly good job.

Fix hyphenation

W   Don't break this word

Ʌ̄   Break word at cursor position

⁻W   Don't break words that follow hyphens or dashes

w.¶   Don't break last word in paragraph

ww.¶   Keep last two words in paragraph together

://| Make URLs and pathnames breakable

o⁻h   Remove optional hyphens

s⁻h   Remove spurious hyphens

   Apply hyphenation exceptions list

   Edit hyphenation exceptions list

The function of most of these hyphenation options is obvious. Some of them, however, need explanation.

Don't break this word

If you select a word and then click this option, Microsoft Word sets the language of the selected word to "No Proofing"—which also means that the word will not be automatically hyphenated or break over a line. This is important for words that shouldn't be broken, such as *women, table,* and *Bible.* If you also use the feature that converts directly applied formatting (such as italic) to character styles, this "No Proofing" will be marked with a "No Break" character style for use in InDesign.

Break word at cursor position

This feature inserts an optional hy¬phen into a word at the spot you have placed your cursor. (CTRL HYPHEN does the same thing.) Then, if Word's automatic hy¬phen¬a¬tion is turned on and the word is going to break over a line, the word will be broken at the spot you've specified. Microsoft Word generally does a good job of breaking words at ends of lines, but sometimes it needs a little help. Note that you can specify more than one possible breaking point in a word. As a bonus, those optional hyphens are retained in InDesign.

Make URLs and pathnames breakable

If your document is destined for typesetting in InDesign or QuarkXPress, you may want to make URLs and pathnames in the text breakable at the end of a line. For example, if your document contained some text like the Editorium URL *http://www.editorium.com,* that text wouldn't ordinarily break at the end of the line, which is why it ends up on this page. This feature inserts *no-width* spaces into such text at logical breaking points, allowing it to break if necessary, like this: *http:// www.editorium.com.* But if the same text *doesn't* come at the end of a line, it will still display correctly: *http://www.editorium.com.* Note that this is *only* for text that will be printed, just to keep things looking nice. If your document will be distributed electronically, with URLs and pathnames set as hyperlinks, you won't want to use this feature, as the no-width spaces could prevent hyperlinks from working.

Many thanks to Wordmeister Steve Hudson for the technology that makes this work.

Remove optional hyphens

This feature removes any optional hyphens you've inserted with the previous feature—or that someone else has inserted.

Remove spurious hyphens

At some point, you've probably had to edit text that has been pasted from a typesetting program and has hy-phens where that program broke words (as in the word *hyphens* on the previous line). You can catch most of these (not all) with Word's spell checker, but it can be a long, tedious process. This feature fixes them for you, and quickly, too.

Sometimes this feature may remove hyphens that you want to keep, such as those in *well-being* or *decision-maker.* That's because the feature relies on Microsoft Word's spell-checker to identify spurious hyphens. It works like this:

1. Find a hyphenated word, such as *well-being.*
2. Remove the hyphen: *wellbeing.*
3. Check the spelling of the word without the hyphen.

If the spell-checker considers the unhyphenated word to be correct, then the feature leaves the word as unhyphenated, which will be the case with *wellbeing* and *decisionmaker,* as Word's spell-checker considers them to be correct. You can see this for yourself by spell-checking a document with those words in it.

The workaround for this problem is to tell Word that *wellbeing* and *decisionmaker* are *not* correctly spelled. The way to do that is to find Word's "exclude dictionary" for your language (e.g., English) and locale (e.g., U.S.), open it in NotePad or some other text editor, and add the words you want to exclude from the spell-checker, each on its own line, like this:

    wellbeing
    decisionmaker

The exclude dictionary for American English is named ExcludeDictionaryEN409.lex. On my computer, it's located here:

    C:\Users\edito\AppData\Roaming\Microsoft\UProof

After you've saved and closed the exclude dictionary, you'll need to close and restart Word for the changes to take effect. At that point, this feature will no longer consider the hyphens in *well-being* and *decision-maker* to be spurious and will leave those words alone while still removing the spurious hyphen in, for example, *sub-stitute.*

Apply hyphenation exceptions list

A hyphenation exceptions list is a list of words that specifies how certain words should (or should not) be broken at the end of a line. For example, a tiny hyphenation exception list might include the following entries as words that shouldn't be broken at all:

    people
    little
    create

It might also include the following words, with hyphens indicating acceptable breaking points:

    con-vert-ible
    tan-gible
    tri-angle

By default, Microsoft Word breaks all of those words badly:

    con-ver-ti-ble
    tang-i-ble
    trian-gle

Typesetting programs like Adobe InDesign already have the ability to use a hyphenation exception list. Now you can use one in Microsoft Word. Editor's ToolKit Plus comes with a list created especially for Word, but you should modify it as needed. The list is called *HyphenationExceptionsList.docx,* and it should be placed in your default Documents folder, which is where Editor's ToolKit Plus expects to find it. The words on the list are *not* case sensitive. The entry for *people* catches both *people* and *People*; the entry for *tan-gible* catches *tan-gible* as well as *Tan-gible.*

Words on the list without hyphens (such as *people)* will be set to "No Proofing" — which means that the word will not be automatically hyphenated or break over a line. If you also use the feature that converts directly applied formatting (such as italic) to character styles, this "No Proofing" will be marked with a "No Break" character style for use in InDesign.

Words on the list with hyphens (such as *con-vert-ible*) will have their hyphens replaced with optional hyphens, so the words will be broken using the hyphenation you've specified rather than Microsoft Word's default. Again, the optional hyphens will be retained in InDesign.

Edit hyphenation exceptions list

If the file *HyphenationExceptionsList.docx* exists in your default Documents folder, this feature opens it so you can edit it. If it doesn't exist, Editor's ToolKit Plus offers to create it for you, including a few sample entries.

NoteStripper

NoteStripper provides a variety of tools for working with notes. Using NoteStripper, you can:

- Strip Word's embedded, automatically numbered footnotes or endnotes to the bottom of a document (or section) as numbered text.
- Strip text notes at the bottom of a document into embedded footnotes or endnotes.
- Strip delimited text to notes—text inside of HTML tags, for example.
- Strip embedded footnotes or endnotes into parenthetical text.
- Strip parenthetical text into embedded footnotes or endnotes.

NoteStripper also includes a utility to check for nested parentheses before stripping parenthetical text into notes. In addition, it makes the following built-in Microsoft Word features easily accessible:

- Convert footnotes to endnotes.
- Convert endnotes to footnotes.
- Swap footnotes and endnotes.
- Convert a selected note to a footnote or endnote.

Stripping notes to text

You may know that it is possible to turn embedded notes into text simply by saving a document in text format. A disadvantage of doing so is that all character formatting is lost. Because notes typically contain book titles in italic, this is a serious problem— thus the need for a program that will strip embedded notes to text while leaving their formatting intact.

Note: If you've deleted notes with Revision Tracking turned on, NoteStripper will delete those notes before stripping notes to text. In other words, it will accept and make permanent your revisions for those notes. If it didn't, the semi-deleted notes would cause problems. NoteStripper will, however, leave your other tracked revisions intact, but it will not track the revisions it makes itself (for example, stripping notes to text).

NoteStripper strips out notes in order from the beginning to the end of a document. That means if all of your chapters are in a single section in a long document, the notes will be stripped and numbered consecutively throughout the document and not within each individual chapter. If you want your notes to be numbered starting with 1 in each chapter, you'll need to separate your chapters with section breaks or put each chapter into an individual document.

To strip notes to text, click the *NoteStripper* icon and then click *Notes to text.*

NoteStripper options

NoteStripper presents you with certain options about how it will run.

Notes to strip

The first option lets you choose the type of note to strip:

- Footnotes.
- Endnotes.
- Both footnotes and endnotes. You'll usually want to use this option.

If you choose both footnotes and endnotes, NoteStripper will convert your endnotes to footnotes and then strip all of the notes together. If you try to strip footnotes first and then strip endnotes later, you'll end up with duplicate note numbers in your document, which you don't want. I've included the option to strip footnotes or endnotes separately, however, for the day when, for some reason, you need to do so. If I know publishing, that day will come sometime.

To location

The second item lets you specify the location where you want the notes to go. You can place them in these locations:

- End of document or section. If your document doesn't have sections, this option will correctly strip notes to the end of your document. Otherwise, it will strip them to the ends of the sections containing the notes, with note numbering restarting in each section.
- End of document only. This option strips notes *only* to the end of the document and *not* to the ends of sections.

Note number format

The third item specifies the numbering style to use in the extracted notes:

- Arabic number followed by a period and a space.
- Roman numeral followed by a period and a space.
- A letter followed by period and a space.
- A symbol followed by a space (used in traditional, handset type).

Please note: NoteStripper turns off revision tracking while it works.

NoteStripper will ask which documents you would like it to work on:

- The active document.
- All open documents.
- All documents in a folder.

Choose the option that fits your needs.

Stripping text to notes

Stripping text to notes means transforming text notes at the end of a document into "embedded" Word footnotes or endnotes—the kind you get by clicking the *Insert* menu, clicking *Footnote,* and selecting the other note options you want to use. Embedded notes are easy to edit because they automatically renumber—you don't have to change note numbers by hand if you delete notes or add them. In addition, if you have a mass of typed notes that are misnumbered, stripping text notes to embedded ones numbers the notes consecutively as they should be, which may be the prime reason for using this feature.

Definitions

To keep things clear, here are definitions for several terms that are used in the instructions that follow:

> *Body text:* The main text of your document.
> *Note reference:* A superscript character in body text that refers to a note.
> *Note:* A footnote or endnote.
> *Note number:* The number at the beginning of a note. (Not to be confused with a note reference.)
> *Note text:* The text of a footnote or endnote.

Here is a sample "document" that contains all of these elements:

This is body text, followed by a note reference.[1]

1. This is a note. It begins with a note number and contains note text.

Rules for stripping text to notes

Before stripping text notes to embedded notes, you must make sure your document follows certain rules:

- *It must have the same number of notes and note references.* If the number of notes and references appears to be different, the program will tell you, and you'll have to fix the problem before the program will run. Possible problems include:

- Some of your note references are formatted as raised rather than superscript, so NoteStripper doesn't see them as references.
- Some of your notes are preceded by a tab or a space. If so, NoteStripper won't see them as notes and so won't count them.
- Whoever typed the note numbers (not references) sometimes used ells for ones.
- If your document has sections, some of the notes are at the end of a section rather than at the end of the document. *All notes must be at the end of the document,* with no other text following. If instead they're at the ends of sections, you'll need to cut and paste them at the end of your document in their proper order before proceeding. Using the Spike feature makes this easy.

- *Note references must be formatted as superscript, either directly or with a character style, or with the Footnote Reference or Endnote Reference character style.* If they're formatted not as one of those but as raised text (or something else), the program won't work. If you need to, you can use FileCleaner to find raised formatting and replace it with superscript formatting before using the program. (Note references don't have to be numbers; they can also be letters or other characters. They cannot, however, be embedded note reference numbers, which are not actually numbers but rather a special code.)

- *If you tell the program to find note numbers formatted as superscript (see "How to strip text to notes," below), nothing but note references must be formatted as superscript in your document's body text.* This is because the program sees any other superscript body text (as in "1st" or "2nd" or "3rd" or "4th") as a note reference. Your note *numbers,* however, can be superscript without causing any problems. If you tell the program to find note references formatted as Footnote Reference or Endnote Reference character styles (see "How to Strip Text to Notes," below), then you don't have to worry about this.

- *Note references must be positioned in your text where you want the embedded notes to be.* In other words, the embedded notes will be placed where the note references initially appeared.
- *The notes must be the last thing in the document.* They must follow the body text at the end of a document, and they can't have other text following them at the end of a document. If they do, the program will see that text as part of the last note.
- *Each note must begin with a note number, include some note text, and end with a carriage return.* A note *cannot* begin with a space, tab, or other non-numerical character. Numbers only! Otherwise, NoteStripper has no way to recognize a note as a note. (You can search for problem notes with the code string ^p^w^# using Word's Find feature. This will find any number preceded by a tab or space preceded by a carriage return.) A single note may, of course, include more than one paragraph.
- *Note numbers must be composed of numbers: 1, 2, 3, 4, 5, 6, 7, 8, 9,* and *0.* Letters and other characters will not work because the program sees them as note text, not as part of a note number.
- *Note numbers must be followed by a period, a space, or a tab (or a combination thereof).* If they're not, NoteStripper will tell you so and select the offending number so you can identify and correct it.

Fortunately, most reasonably formatted documents already follow these rules. That means you may not have to do anything to your document before stripping text to notes. However, it doesn't hurt to look over a document and make sure that the rules have been followed.

Note numbers can have any formatting, including superscript, and they can have any number of digits. Also, you can have as many notes as you want. Finally, your document can include notes that are already embedded. The new notes will be stripped in with the existing notes where they belong.

Here is an example of a document that would work properly:

This is body text.[1] This is body[2] text. This is body text.[3]

    1. This is note text.
    2. This is note text.
    3. This is note text.

Here's another example, using superscript note numbers followed by a space:

This is body text.[1] This is body[2] text. This is body text.[3]

    [1] This is note text.
    [2] This is note text.
    [3] This is note text.

And believe it or not, this example would also work just fine because it follows the rules above, however strange it may look:

This is body text.[54] This is body[abc] text. This is body text.[2]

    14.This is note text.
    3 This is note text.
    [22] This is note text.

In each of these cases, after stripping text to notes, you'd get a document that had the notes embedded and automatically renumbered. The document would look like this (with the notes embedded, of course):

This is body text.[1] This is body[2] text. This is body text.[3]

    1. This is note text.
    2. This is note text.
    3. This is note text.

How to strip text to notes

To strip text to notes, follow these steps:

1. Open the document in which you want to strip text to notes.
2. Place your cursor at the beginning of the notes, which must be at the *end* of your document. (This is so important that the program will ask if you have done it. If you haven't, but you say you have, the program will see any paragraph beginning with a number [like this paragraph] as a note and report that you have unmatched notes and note references.)
3. Click the *NoteStripper* icon.
4. Click *Text to notes.*

The following dialog will be displayed:

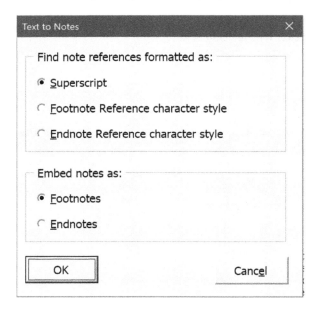

Select the options you want to use. You can have the program look for note references formatted as superscript, Footnote Reference character style, or Endnote Reference character style. Which one you choose, of course, depends on how the note references are actually formatted in your document. Usually, they will simply be superscript, and even if they're formatted with one of the character styles, they are still likely to be superscript. Let's say, however, that they're formatted with one of the character styles, and you tell the program to find note references formatted with that style. Then your document can contain superscript text *other than note references* without warning you that note references and note numbers don't match. Please note, too, that NoteStripper's Notes to Text feature (see above) formats note references *in the character styles* and not just as superscript.

After the program runs, your typed notes will be embedded as automatically numbered Word notes. Then, if you like, you can use Word's note options to change numbering schemes, formatting, and so on. See your Word documentation for more information.

Stripping delimited text to notes

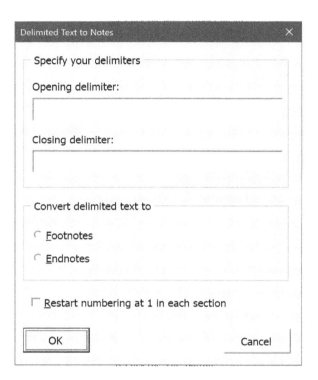

On occasion, you may encounter documents with notes included as inline text in some kind of delimiters, <<like this.>> You can use NoteStripper to turn such notes into true embedded footnotes or endnotes. Tagged text from typesetting programs—Ventura, for example—often includes delimited notes, as do many public-domain texts available on the Internet. To use this feature:

1. Click the *NoteStripper* menu.
2. Click *Delimited text to notes*.
3. Specify the documents you want to use.
4. In the dialog box, enter the beginning and ending delimiters used with your inline notes. You can use Word's wildcard Find codes in these boxes if you need to. For example, you can use ^013 to specify a carriage return and ^t to specify a tab.
5. Select footnotes or endnotes.
6. If your document contains more than one section, you can tell the program to restart numbering at 1 in each section. If you don't select this option, notes will be numbered consecutively throughout the document.
7. Click the *OK* button.

NoteStripper will ask which documents you would like it to work on:

- The active document.
- All open documents.
- All documents in a folder.

Choose the option that fits your needs.

This feature uses Word's wildcard searching to find delimiters, so if you have certain characters in your delimiters, you'll need to "escape" those characters by preceding them with a backward slash. For example, you'd escape an opening parenthesis like this:

\(

And you'd escape a typesetting code like this:

\<I\>

Here are the characters that need to be escaped:

( ) [ ] { } < > ? ! @ * ^ \

That's the bad news; the good news is that you can actually use Word's wildcards to specify delimiters. For more information, see my *Wildcard Cookbook for Microsoft Word* (ISBN 978-1-4341-0398-7).

Stripping notes to parenthetical citations

In some documents you may decide that source citations should appear in parentheses rather than in footnotes or endnotes. In that case, you can use NoteStripper to strip out Word's embedded notes and place the note text in parentheses where the note references used to be. You can do this with footnotes, endnotes, or both. To do so:

1. Click the *NoteStripper* menu.
2. Click *Notes to parenthetical text.*
3. Answer the questions on your screen.

Your notes will be converted into parenthetical citations.

After the program is finished, you may want to go through your document to see if some of the citations should be in brackets rather than in parentheses. This would be true if the program placed a parenthetical citation at the end of text that is already in parentheses, or if your notes already contained publication information in parentheses. I've provided a utility program to help you solve this problem. To run the program, click *Check for nested parentheses* under the *NoteStripper* menu. The program will identify the first nested parentheses it sees. Then it will stop so you can fix them. To find more nested parentheses, run the program again.

Stripping parenthetical citations into notes

In some documents you may decide that source citations should appear in footnotes or endnotes rather than in parentheses in the document's body text. In that case, you can use NoteStripper to strip out the parenthetical citations and turn them into Word's embedded, automatically numbered footnotes or endnotes. To do so, position your cursor at the place in your document where you want the program to start. Then:

1. Click the *NoteStripper* menu.
2. Click *Parenthetical text to notes.*

The program will ask you to choose the type of notes you want to convert:

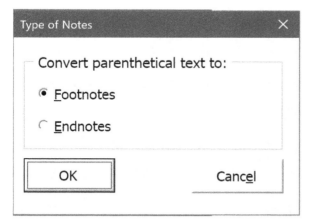

Click the option you want, then click *OK.*

Next, the program will ask you to choose the type of *entries* you want to convert:

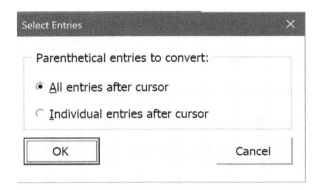

Click the option you want, then click *OK.*

Note: The program does *not* work from the beginning of the document; it works from wherever your cursor is currently positioned.

All entries after cursor automatically finds and changes all parenthetical text after your cursor position.

Individual entries after cursor finds each occurrence of parenthetical text separately and presents you with several options. You can:

- Convert the current entry.
- Skip to the next entry, leaving the current entry untouched.
- Undo the previous conversion.
- Convert all remaining entries from the cursor position to the end of the document.
- Cancel the program at the current cursor position.

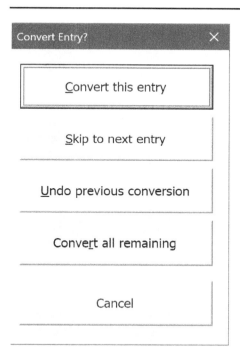

Converting entries individually takes longer than having the program do them all automatically, but it allows you to preserve parenthetical text that should *not* be turned into a note (like this). If you're certain that everything in parentheses should be turned into a note, click *All entries after cursor.*

If you have only a few places where parentheses should be preserved, and you know where they are, you could manually change them into something like three "at" signs: @@@. Then you could have NoteStripper automatically convert the other parenthetical citations. Finally, you could go back and change all occurrences of three "at" signs into the proper parentheses.

Transposing reference numbers and punctuation

Stripping parenthetical text to notes automatically transposes certain punctuation with note references. For example, if parenthetical text was formatted the way it appears after this sentence, the text of the note would ordinarily be embedded without a final period because the text inside the parentheses has no period (Lyon, *Using NoteStripper,* p. 10). In addition, the reference number would appear to the left of the sentence's period, like this[1]. To fix that problem, the program transposes each reference number with punctuation that follows it, specifically:

- Periods.
- Commas.
- Question marks.
- Exclamation marks.

Depending on how your parenthetical citations are punctuated, however, the program may not fix them perfectly. After running the macro, you'll need to look at your notes to make sure they're punctuated to your liking.

Converting notes

Buried deep in Microsoft Word's *References* menu are three commands that allow you to convert footnotes to endnotes and vice versa. You can convert notes in selected text or in an entire document. I've included these commands on the *NoteStripper* menu for easy access. They include:

- *Convert Footnotes.* This command converts footnotes to endnotes.
- *Convert Endnotes.* This command converts endnotes to footnotes.
- *Swap Notes.* This command converts footnotes to endnotes and endnotes to footnotes.

Editor's ToolKit Plus provides an additional feature for turning footnotes to endnotes or vice versa:

- *Convert Notes.* This command converts *selected* notes to either footnotes or endnotes. Your cursor must actually be in the note text for this to occur.

ListFixer

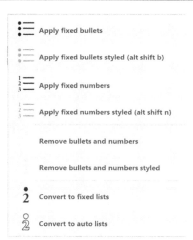

Apply fixed bullets

Apply fixed bullets styled (alt shift b)

Apply fixed numbers

Apply fixed numbers styled (alt shift n)

Remove bullets and numbers

Remove bullets and numbers styled

Convert to fixed lists

Convert to auto lists

Microsoft Word's automatically numbered and bulleted lists are hard to understand, unpredictable, and, worst of all, don't use real characters. That's why I've created ListFixer, which converts automatic numbers and bullets into *real* numbers and bullets in the active document, all open documents, or all documents in a folder. In addition, it can be used instead of the Bullets and Numbering icons on Word's Ribbon interface.

ListFixer can also apply special paragraph styles to your lists, allowing you to adjust indentation, line spacing, and tab alignment for list items by modifying the styles.

If you've applied automatic numbering and bullets with paragraph styles, you can have ListFixer duplicate those styles, without the automatic numbering and bullets, and apply real numbers and bullets to the paragraphs instead—thus allowing you to maintain the formatting of those paragraphs.

Finally, although I hesitate to admit it, ListFixer can *unfix* your lists, if you so desire. In other words, if you have lists with real numbers and bullets but want to convert them to automatically numbered and bulleted lists, ListFixer will do the job, for the active document, all open documents, or all documents in a folder.

ListFixer is purposely *not* smart when used with selected text. If you apply numbers to text under a previously numbered list, it will *not* number your selection as a continuation of the list above it, nor will it try to guess what the next number should be in a list after a "skipped" paragraph. Why? So that *you,* rather than Microsoft Word, are in control. If you need to continue numbering after a previously numbered paragraph, select the *entire* list and have ListFixer apply your numbers. And if you need to type a few numbers in by hand, you can, because all of the numbers created by ListFixer are real characters rather than invisible, ephemeral, uncontrollable codes inserted by Microsoft Word.

When fixing *all* of the automatic lists in a document, however, ListFixer *is* smart. If a list starts with 7, for example, ListFixer fixes that number as 7 and not as 1. In addition, ListFixer is perfectly capable of fixing multilevel, mixed-format lists created as automatic lists in Microsoft Word. That means if you need to create a complex, multilevel list, you can do so with Word's automatic list features and then convert the numbers and letters at the beginning of list items to fixed numbers and letters using ListFixer.

ListFixer has several advantages over public-domain macros that convert automatic lists to fixed lists:

- It includes batch processing so you can automatically convert all lists in all active documents or all documents in a folder rather than one document at a time.
- When converting bullets, it leaves all other Symbol characters intact.
- If you like, it will style the list paragraphs for easy, flexible formatting.
- It allows you to apply real bullets or numbers to *selected* text.

If you use paragraph styles to apply bullets or numbers, ListFixer duplicates and applies the existing styles but without *automatic* bullets or numbers, thus preserving existing formatting. This makes it possible to convert complex, multilevel lists.

Using ListFixer

Click the *ListFixer* menu to see the various features the program has to offer:

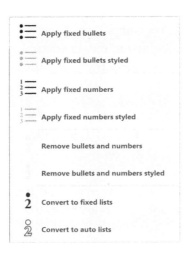

You can even use these features on *existing* lists, whether the numbering and bullets are automatic or not. For example, you could apply fixed bullets to a previously numbered list to remove the numbers and apply bullets instead.

Apply fixed bullets

Apply fixed bullets inserts a bullet followed by a tab in front of each paragraph of selected text.

Apply fixed bullets styled

Apply fixed bullets styled inserts a bullet followed by a tab in front of each paragraph of selected text, then applies a paragraph style named Bullet List to each paragraph.

If the style Bullet List already exists in a document, ListFixer will not re-create it; it will use the style already defined. Using Apply Fixed Bullets with an already-styled list will *not* remove the styles, because ListFixer has no way of knowing what style you want to apply instead. But you can easily select the list and apply any style you like. Note that if the bullet doesn't exist in the font used in the style, you'll end up with little blank squares rather than bullets.

You can also use this feature with the keyboard shortcut ALT SHIFT B.

Apply fixed numbers

Apply fixed numbers inserts a number followed by a period and a tab in front of each paragraph of selected text.

Apply fixed numbers styled

Apply fixed numbers styled inserts a number followed by a period and a tab in front of each paragraph of selected text, then applies paragraph style named Number List to each paragraph. You can also use this feature with the keyboard shortcut ALT SHIFT N.

If the style Number List already exists in a document, ListFixer does not re-create it. Instead, it uses the style already defined. Using Apply Fixed Numbers with an already-styled list does *not* remove the styles, because ListFixer has no way of knowing what style you want to apply instead. But you can easily select the list and apply any style you like.

Remove bullets and numbers

Remove Bullets and Numbers removes bullets and numbers (manual or automatic) from selected text.

Remove bullets and numbers styled

Remove bullets and numbers styled removes bullets and numbers (manual or automatic) from selected text. In addition, unlike ListFixer's other features, it *does* apply the Normal paragraph style (to remove list paragraph styles applied earlier). If you don't use Normal as your default style, you may want to apply some other style to the selected list.

Convert to fixed lists

Convert to Fixed Lists converts all automatic numbers and bullets into manual numbers and bullets in the active document, all open documents, or all documents in a folder. This feature does not track revisions, as it simply *converts* automatic lists to fixed lists rather than applying lists to begin with.

Convert to auto lists

Convert to Auto Lists converts manual numbers and bullets into automatic numbers and bullets in the active document, all open documents, or all documents in a folder. This feature does not track revisions, as it simply *converts* fixed lists to automatic lists rather than applying lists to begin with.

NOTE: This feature expects list numbers to be an actual number followed by a period and then a space or a tab. If your numbers take some other format (such as a number followed by a closing parenthesis), this feature will not work correctly.

MegaReplacer

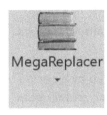

MegaReplacer finds and replaces multiple text strings (characters, words, or phrases), text formatting (such as bold or italic), or styles (such as Heading 1) in multiple documents. You can use MegaReplacer to do such things as replace common misspellings throughout a manuscript or change a character's name in the chapters of a novel.

MegaReplacer is like dynamite: very powerful and thus very useful—and very dangerous if used carelessly, as it *will* make all the changes in all the documents exactly the way you tell it to. I strongly recommend that you try MegaReplacer several times on a variety of test documents until you understand fully how it works and what it can do, and that you *back up your documents* before using it.

Creating a master list for replacing text

Before using MegaReplacer to replace text, you'll need to prepare a "master list" of the text you want to replace. (To replace text formatting only [such as bold or italic], no master list is needed.)

In previous versions of MegaReplacer, entries on a master list were a rather arcane sequence of text strings and commands that looked something like this:

occurrance|occurrence
millenium|millennium
Department|department+c
per|according to+w
p ([0-9]@.\))|p. \1+m

But no more. A master list is now an easy-to-use table that looks like this:

FIND	Format	REPLACE	Format	Highlight	Option	Comment
!!!!		!				
!!!		!				
!!		!				
%		percent				
&		and				
accidently		accidentally				
accomodate		accommodate				
accomodation		accommodation				
accordian		accordion				
acknowledgement		acknowledgment				
acquaintence		acquaintance				
adjacent to		next to				
albeit		though				
all of the		all the				
alot		a lot			w	
alright		all right				
amidst		amid				
amongst		among				

In addition, MegaReplacer can now find and replace text with formatting (bold, italic, etc.) and styles (Heading 1, Block, etc.). It can also mark found items with highlighting in ten different colors so you can check those items later as you work.

For those who have existing master lists, MegaReplacer includes utilities to convert those lists to the new table format.

To create a master list for text:

1. Click the MegaReplacer menu.
2. Click "Create master list for text."

MegaReplacer will create a new document that includes the table that will hold your entries. For each entry, type the text to find in the "FIND" column and the text's replacement in the "REPLACE" column. You must be *absolutely accurate* in typing the entries the way you want them. The entries can be the same length as a regular Word find or replace string: from 1 to 255 characters. You can have from 1 to 8,142 entries.

Using comments in a master list

You can add comments about your entries in the "Comments" column on the right side of the table. These comments are for your own reference and convenience—MegaReplacer will simply ignore them. You can also add more expansive comments on their own lines above and below the table.

Using Word's find options

When replacing text, you can use Word's basic Find options just as you can with Word's regular Find feature. These options are:

- Match Case.
- Find Whole Words Only.
- Use Pattern Matching (Use Wildcards).
- Sounds Like.
- Match All Word Forms.

To use these options, enter one of the following codes into the "Option" column on the table:

c	Match Case
w	Find Whole Words Only
&	Match Case and Find Whole Words Only at the same time
m	Use Pattern Matching (Use Wildcards)
l	Sounds Like
a	Match All Word Forms

You can use only one of these options per entry.

Please note that with MegaReplacer, you can't use Word's Find options to do anything you couldn't ordinarily do when searching manually. For example, using Word's Find feature manually, you can try searching a document for a carriage return (^p) with "Use Wildcards" turned on. If you do, Word will give you an error message. MegaReplacer won't give you an error message, but it also won't find the carriage return. In effect, it will simply ignore that find-and-replace entry. Similarly, if you put several words separated by spaces in Word's "Find What" box, the "Find Whole Words Only" option is unavailable. This is also true with MegaReplacer, even though you can't *see* that it is unavailable. If you have any questions about whether a find-and-replace entry will work with a certain option, you should try it manually in Word. If it won't work that way, it won't work with MegaReplacer either.

Finding and replacing formatting

You can find and replace formatted text by using the following codes in the "Format" columns of the table:

bo	bold
it	italic
ul	underline
st	strikethrough
sp	superscript
sb	subscript
sc	small caps
ac	all caps
s:stylename	style (for example, s:Heading 1)

Highlighting

You can highlight replaced text using the following codes in the "Highlight" column of the table:

A   gray
B   blue
D   dark yellow
E   teal
G   green
P   pink
R   red
T   turquoise
V   violet
Y   yellow

Creating a master list for replacing styles

You can use MegaReplacer to replace one style with another. For example, if you have headings styled as Heading 1 but need to style them as Title instead, MegaReplacer will do that for you. Before using MegaReplacer to replace styles, you'll need to prepare a "master list" of the styles you want to replace. To do:

1. Click the MegaReplacer menu.
2. Click "Create master list for styles."

MegaReplacer will create a new document that includes the table that will hold your entries. For each entry, type the name of the style to find in the "FIND style" column and the style's replacement in the "REPLACE style" column. You must be *absolutely accurate* in typing the entries the way you want them. You can include comments in the "Comment" column. You can have from 1 to 8,142 entries.

Please note that MegaReplacer can't find or replace styles that don't actually *exist* in your documents. In addition, it can't find or replace styles that have been misspelled in your master list, which must be absolutely accurate.

Running MegaReplacer

Save your master list with a name of your choice but leave it open on the screen as the active document. Click the *MegaReplacer* icon and select *MegaReplacer.* The following dialog will be displayed:

What would you like to replace?

MegaReplacer asks whether you want to replace text, text formatting, or styles. To find and replace text formatting only (such as bold or italic), no master list is needed.

How would you like to work?

You can elect to replace automatically or to approve individual replacements.

Replace Automatically

If you elect to replace automatically, MegaReplacer will make all of your replacements in the documents you specified without further intervention from you. Use this option for items you *know* will always need to be changed, such as a list of common misspellings. For example, your list could include accommodate/accommodate, supercede/supersede, millenium/millennium, and so on. For more examples, see the document named "Automatic Corrections.docx" that came with Editor's ToolKit Plus in the "Goodies" folder.

Approve Individual Replacements

Use this option for items that *may* need to be replaced. The word *impact,* for example, can be used as a verb or a noun, but many editors avoid leaving it as a verb, using *affect* instead. For more examples, see the document named "Other Possible Corrections.docx" that came with Editor's ToolKit Plus in the "Goodies" folder.

If you elect to approve individual replacements, you'll have the following choices each time the program finds something to replace:

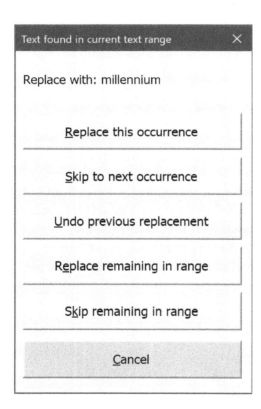

- *Replace this occurrence* replaces the text that was found with the new text you specified.
- *Skip to next occurrence* skips the text that was found and searches for the next occurrence.

- *Undo previous replacement* undoes the last replacement you approved.
- *Replace remaining in range* replaces the remaining occurrences in the current text range (main document, footnotes, endnotes, etc.).
- *Skip remaining in range* skips the remaining occurrences in the current text range (main document, footnotes, endnotes, etc.).
- *Cancel* stops MegaReplacer dead in its tracks.

You can use keyboard shortcuts for each of these. In fact, all you have to do is press the letter that is underlined on each button. For example, to "Replace this occurrence," just press the *R* key on your keyboard. To "Skip to next occurrence," press the *S* key. And so on.

If you prefer, you can also use these keys in combination with the ALT key. Once you do that, however, you can no longer use the individual keys *without* combining them with ALT, at least not during the current session.

What documents would you like to use?

If you're replacing *text* or *styles,* you can run MegaReplacer on:

- The first document after your master list. This is the document that would be active if you closed the master list. Be careful to get the right document. Better yet, open only *one* document besides your master list so that you don't accidentally run MegaReplacer on the wrong one.
- All open documents except your master list.
- All documents in a folder—*unless* you've opted to approve individual replacements, in which case only the first two options are available. Otherwise, various problems ensue, so we're going to avoid the whole issue.

If you're replacing text *formatting* only, you can run MegaReplacer on:

- The active document.
- All open documents.
- All documents in a folder.

Finding and replacing text formatting only

"Text formatting" means the following directly applied formatting:

- Bold
- Italic
- Underline
- Strikethrough
- Superscript
- Subscript
- Small caps
- All caps

If you choose this option, the Text Formatting dialog appears. Putting a black check into a dialog checkbox tells MegaReplacer to find or replace that kind of formatting. Putting a gray check makes MegaReplacer neutral toward that kind of formatting. Leaving a checkbox blank tells MegaReplacer *not* to find or replace that kind of formatting. For example, consider the following selections:

Under "Find What," bold is turned on, italic is turned on, underline is turned off, and the other formats are left neutral. In this case, MegaReplacer will find text that is bold *and* italic but *not* bold italic underline. It will *not* find text that is bold but not italic, or text that is italic but not bold. It will, however, find text that is bold italic strikethrough, bold italic superscript, and so on. If this isn't clear, try experimenting with some junk text in the active document. You'll soon understand how the process works. Basically, it corresponds to the formatting options in Word's Find and Replace dialogs, where you can set the "Find What" box to bold, italic, and *not* underline, leaving all other formatting unspecified (to continue with our example).

Under "Replace With," strikethrough is turned on and all caps and small caps are turned off, which means that found formatting will be replaced with strikethrough but *not* all caps or small caps. That means if something in bold italic not underline *all caps* or *small caps* is found, it will be replaced with strikethrough *not* all caps or small caps. Keeping track of all these options can be complicated, but they give you enormous control over how you find and replace text formatting.

MegaReplacer remembers your formatting choices from session to session. To reset all checkboxes to gray (neutral), click the *No formatting* button. You can also reset each option individually.

Performing previous Find and Replace on multiple documents

Perform previous Find and Replace on multiple documents takes your previous Find and Replace options (text to find, text to replace, whole words only, formatting, and so on) and performs that Find and Replace on the active document, all open documents, or all documents in a folder. This makes it easy to set up those options with Word's Find and Replace feature as you usually would but then run the options on multiple documents at the same time. Powerful stuff.

Keyboard repeat Find and Replace

This feature also uses the options from your previous Find and Replace operation but does so under your control at the keyboard.

- ALT CTRL SHIFT > = Find again forward.
- ALT CTRL SHIFT < = Find again backward.
- ALT CTRL SHIFT / = Replace the current instance of found text.

Puller

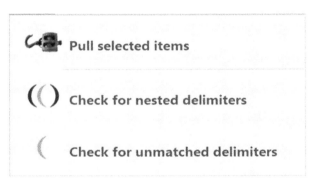

- Pull selected items
- Check for nested delimiters
- Check for unmatched delimiters

Puller copies delimited items (such as bracketed or parenthetical text) from the active document, all open documents, or all documents in a folder. Then it pastes them into a separate document, sorts the entries alphabetically, and deletes duplicate items, providing an alphabetical list of the delimited items you specified. If you need to create a summary of typesetting codes or source citations, you need Puller!

Using Puller

To use Puller, follow these steps:

1. Click the *Puller* menu at the top of your Word window.
2. Click *Puller.*
3. Select the options you want to use.
4. Click *OK* to continue.

Puller options

You can use Puller to make lists of various kinds of delimited items, including:

•   *<Items in angle brackets>*. This option is useful for creating lists of codes in marked-up documents, such as QuarkXPress Tags or HTML codes.
•   *(Items in parentheses).* Use this option to create a list of parenthetical source citations, which you can then use in checking consistency, creating a bibliography, and so on. If you have Puller eliminate duplicate items, and you then see what appear to be two identical items on the list, you can be sure that they're different in some way. If you can figure out what that is, you've removed one more inconsistency from your manuscript.
•   *[Items in square brackets].* I'm not sure what you might have in square brackets, but this option will pull them!
•   *Other delimited items.* Use this option to specify custom delimiters, such as braces, slashes, or pipe symbols. You can even use multiple characters or codes, like <I> and <\I> or <para> and <endpara>. Note, however, that Puller uses Word's wildcard searching to find delimiters, so if you use certain characters in your custom delimiters, you'll need to "escape" those characters by preceding them with a backward slash. For example, you'd escape an opening parenthesis like this:

```
\(
```

And you'd escape a typesetting code like this:

```
\<I\>
```

Here are the characters that need to be escaped:

```
( ) [ ] { } < >  ? ! @  *  ^  \
```

That's the bad news; the good news is that you can actually use Word's wildcards to specify delimiters. For more information, see my *Wildcard Cookbook for Microsoft Word* (ISBN 978-1-4341-0398-7).

Puller includes many other options of items to pull from your manuscript into a new, blank document. They include:

- Text styled as (choose a style from a dropdown list).
- Comments.
- Tracked revisions.
- Bookmarked text.
- Highlighted text.
- Misspellings.
- Grammar problems.
- Headings.
- Graphics.
- Equations.
- Acronyms.
- Citations inserted with Word's *Insert Citation* feature.

- Bibliography.
- Index entries.

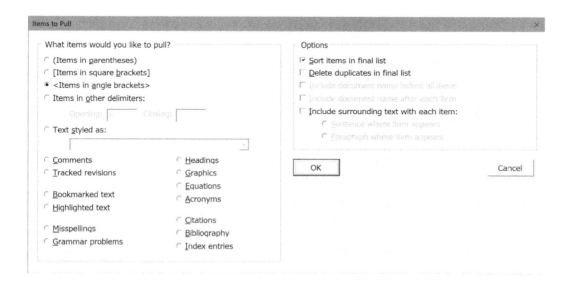

If you need to pull any such items for later reference or for someone else to review, now you can.

Options

You can have Puller do various things to the items pulled:

- Sort items in final list.
- Delete duplicates in final list.

- Include document name before all items.
- Include document name after each item.
- Include surrounding text with each item (sentence or paragraph).

I was once called upon to testify in a court case involving a copyright dispute over a six-volume novel series. I had to show every paragraph in which one of the main characters was mentioned. It would have taken hours to go through the Word documents, copy each paragraph that included the character's name, and paste that paragraph into a different document. I used MegaReplacer to enclose every occurrence of the character's name in angle brackets. Then Puller took less than a minute to pull every paragraph that included the bracketed name.

Documents to work on

You can select whether to run Puller on:

- The active document.
- All open documents.
- All documents in a folder.

Puller automatically works on every text range in a document (main text, footnotes, etc.).

Utilities

Puller comes with two utility programs:

- Check for unmatched delimiters.
- Check for nested delimiters.

Check for unmatched delimiters checks for unmatched delimiters in the active document. For example, if it finds an opening parenthesis but not a closing one, it will let you know. Then you can fix the problem before running Puller.

Check for nested delimiters checks for delimiters within delimiters in the active document. For example, if it finds an opening parenthesis followed by an open parenthesis and then a closing one, it will let you know. Then you can fix the problem before running Puller.

WordCounter

WordCounter counts the number of words, pages, and characters in the active document, all open documents, or all documents in a folder. If you're writing or editing and bill by the word or by the page, you'll find WordCounter indispensable. After it's finished counting, WordCounter presents you with a nicely formatted table with the count for each document you specified and totals for the number of words, pages, and characters in your documents.

Count words

To use WordCounter, follow these steps:

1. Click the *WordCounter* menu at the top of your Word window.
2. Click *Count words*
3. Select the options you want to use.

WordCounter options

WordCounter actually counts any of the following:

- Words.

- Pages as currently formatted.
- Pages calculated as words divided by 250.
- Characters without spaces.
- Characters with spaces.

If you like, it will include footnotes and endnotes in the count. Comments are not included.

Finally, if you so specify, it will create its report in landscape orientation, which is helpful if you're counting many things at once.

List words

You can have WordCounter list all of the words in the active document, all open documents, or all documents in a folder. In addition, you can have it include the number of times each word is used. Comments are not included.

This can be surprisingly useful for editing, allowing you to catch spelling or capitalization variations you might otherwise overlook. It also helps you spot terms that may be overused.

Switcheroo

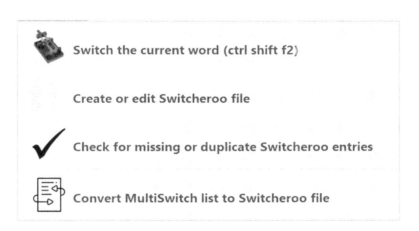

Switch the current word (ctrl shift f2)

Create or edit Switcheroo file

Check for missing or duplicate Switcheroo entries

Convert MultiSwitch list to Switcheroo file

Switcheroo instantly switches between words or phrases using entries from the Switcheroo file (provided). The file does *not* have to be open for Switcheroo to work (although it must be present in your Documents folder).

The Switcheroo file looks like this:

since	because	as			
stationary	stationery				
storey	story				
storeys	stories				
than	then	from			
their	there	they're	they are		
through	threw	thorough	though	thru	
to	too	two			
tortuous	torturous				
toward	towards				

As you can see, the entries are kept in a simple, editable table, with room for six words (or phrases) per row. If the word in your manuscript is capitalized, Switcheroo capitalizes its replacement, even though the word isn't capitalized in the table (although you *can* include words that are capitalized).

Switch the current word

To run Switcheroo, put your cursor anywhere in a word you want to switch. For example, if your client has used "it's" to mean "its," place your cursor in the word "it's" and press CTRL SHIFT F2. The word instantly switches to "its." If you then realize that "it's" was correct after all, press CTRL SHIFT F2 again to switch back. Switcheroo loops through all the words (or phrases) in the row that includes the original word.

Create or edit Switcheroo file

You can use Switcheroo to switch between (or among) commonly confused words, replace contractions with spelled-out words (or vice versa), or even create a specialized thesaurus.

Editor's ToolKit Plus comes with a sample file called "Switcheroo.docx" that includes words and phrases authors sometimes confuse, such as "imply" and "infer" or "loose" and "lose." To see or modify the file, click Text > Switcheroo > Create or edit Switcheroo file.

To add a new word to the file, place your cursor on the word and press CTRL SHIFT F2 (the regular keyboard shortcut to switch words). Switcheroo asks if you'd like to add that word to your Switcheroo file:

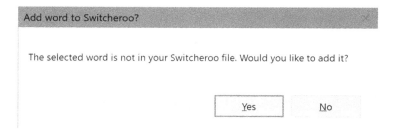

If you add the word, you should also add at least one other word in that row of the table to switch with the original word. Be sure to save the file when you're finished. Again, the file does *not* have to be open for Switcheroo to work.

Check for missing or duplicate Switcheroo entries

This utility checks for missing or duplicate entries in your open Switcheroo list. If your Switcheroo list is fairly long, this utility may take a long time to run, so you should use it only if you're running into weird problems when using Switcheroo. Missing entries will be highlighted in turquoise. Duplicate entries will be highlighted in yellow.

Convert MultiSwitch list to Switcheroo file

This utility converts a MultiSwitch list to a Switcheroo file. You can learn more about Paul Beverley's MultiSwitch macro here:

http://www.archivepub.co.uk/book.html

Why convert? Because, even as useful as it is, MultiSwitch requires you to think like a programmer, providing duplicate entries for capitalized words and reversed duplicates for switching back and forth:

less
fewer

Less
Fewer

that
which

which
that

The same entries for Switcheroo would look like this:

less	fewer
that	which

With Switcheroo, there's no need to repeat word pairs in reverse order or have separate entries for capitalized words.

If you're editing a manuscript that includes dialog (such as fiction), you'll find Switcheroo particularly useful for switching between spelled-out words and contractions:

would not	wouldn't
will not	won't

QuoteMe

QuoteMe includes two features, *Blockify quoted text* and *Quotify blocked text.*

Blockify quoted text

Blockify turns text in quotation marks into block quotations (text styled as Block Text), removing opening and closing marks and converting double marks to single and vice versa as appropriate. Different style manuals recommend different numbers of words to include in a block quotation (*Chicago* says 100 or more), so Blockify lets you specify the number of words to convert.

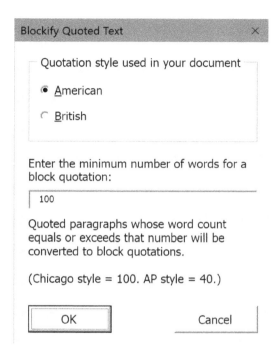

Quotify blocked text

Quotify is like Blockify in reverse. It turns block quotations (text styled as Block Text) into regular text in quotation marks, adding opening and closing marks and converting double marks to single and vice versa as appropriate. Like Blockify, Quotify lets you specify the number of words to convert.

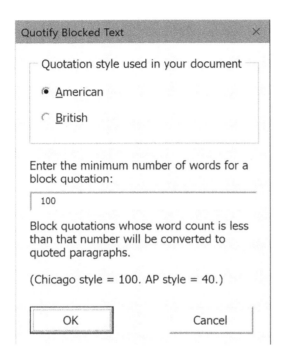

No more manually counting words or eyeballing the number of lines! No more manually styling text as Block Quote or Normal! No more adjusting quotation marks! Blockify and Quotify take care of everything automatically.

Note, however, that there is one circumstance in which it is impossible for a computer program to distinguish (and thus correctly handle) an apostrophe from a single closing quotation mark: When a sentence includes both a single closing quotation mark after an *s* and a plural possessive ending in *s*. Here's an example:

I must explain to you how all this mistaken idea of denouncing pleasures was born, and I will give you a 'complete account of the systems' limits' and expound the actual teachings of the great explorer of the truth.

Which word ends the quotation: *systems'* or *limits'?* There's no way to know, apart from human intervention. For that reason, Blockify and Quotify highlight in green any such cases they don't know how to handle:

I must explain to you how all this mistaken idea of denouncing pleasures was born, and I will give you a "complete account of the systems' limits' and expound the actual teachings of the great explorer of the truth.

You'll need to review these cases and fix them manually as needed. After you're finished, you can use the program's "Remove highlighting" feature to get rid of the green (along with any other highlighting).

Converters

Convert with Pandoc

Convert with Pandoc exports the active document in a different format (such as ePub) using Pandoc, the free and open-source document converter. (You must install Pandoc from pandoc.org to use this feature.) If you need to convert a Word document into, say, Markdown or LaTeX, now you can. You'll find the converted document in the same folder as the original. See Pandoc's documentation for more in-depth information.

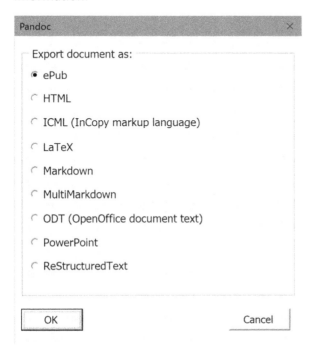

QuarkConverter

In the past several years, the ability of QuarkXPress to import Word documents has markedly improved, so you may no longer need QuarkConverter. But if you're having problems bringing Word documents into QuarkXPress, QuarkConverter offers a good solution, translating Microsoft Word documents into XPress Tag files that can be imported into QuarkXPress almost automatically. This also solves several other problems, all of which are explained below.

QuarkConverter 2015 implemented the ability to import footnotes and endnotes in a Microsoft Word document. Nevertheless, if you're planning to use QuarkConverter with documents that contain Word's automatically numbered footnotes or endnotes, you should first use NoteStripper to strip the notes out as text. Otherwise, QuarkConverter won't convert your notes correctly for QuarkXPress. If you're also going to use FileCleaner to clean up common typographical problems, you should run the programs in this order:

1. FileCleaner.
2. NoteStripper.
3. QuarkConverter.

I *strongly* recommend that you try QuarkConverter several times on a variety of test files, then try importing them into QuarkXPress, until you understand fully how the whole process works.

Understanding QuarkConverter

Unfortunately, when you bring a Word document into QuarkXPress, the imported document retains its formatting, which prevents typesetters from using QuarkXPress as it was meant to be used. One of the beauties of QuarkXPress is that by modifying a document's style sheet, you can globally change the document's format—unless, of course, the document has other formatting applied directly, which is what you get when you bring in a Word document. In that case, you can still change the style sheet, but you'll also have to manually reapply the paragraph styles, which makes little sense. Of course, you could always save your Word document as a text file, losing *all* formatting, then bring it into QuarkXPress and reapply all of the formatting manually. That doesn't sound like a good solution either.

XPress Tag files

The answer to this dilemma is to import documents as XPress Tag files, which are text files that use tags to mark formatting. For example, an XPress Tag file has no italic text. It can't, since it's just a text file. Instead, it includes the tag <I> on each side of an italicized word, and when QuarkXPress sees that tag, it turns on italics. When it sees it again (or sees the <$> tag), it turns them off. Similarly, an XPress Tag file might include the tag @Heading 1: in front of a paragraph that will be a main heading. When QuarkXPress sees that tag, it formats the following text with the characteristics the typesetter has specified for Heading 1 in the document's style sheet.

So how do you get an XPress Tag file? That's where QuarkConverter comes in. QuarkConverter turns Microsoft Word documents into XPress Tag files that can be brought into QuarkXPress, allowing a typesetter to change type specifications globally. For example, let's say you've been editing in Word and have marked spec levels using paragraph styles (which is what you *should* do). You used the style Heading 1 for your main headings and Heading 2 as subheads. When you convert your document with QuarkConverter, those headings will be tagged as @Heading 1: and @Heading 2:. Character styles will be tagged as well. Also, most character *formatting* will be tagged and thus preserved, including bold, italic, underline, word underline, strikethrough, small caps, all caps, superscript, subscript, and raised 3 points. (Such oddities as shadow, outline, double underline, and dotted underline are not supported and will be lost, unless you change them into something else before using QuarkConverter.) QuarkConverter does not convert such formatting as fonts, point size, paragraph formatting, kerning, and so on, all of which should be defined in your QuarkXPress style sheets, not in directly applied formatting.

Character translation

When you start QuarkConverter, it checks to see if you are working on a PC or a Macintosh. Then it asks you to choose the platform on which you will be using QuarkXPress (Macintosh or PC). This is necessary so that QuarkConverter can properly translate members of the ANSI character set numbered above 128, which are different on Mac and PC.

For example, if you have the word *fiancé* in a PC Word document and bring it into QuarkXPress on the Macintosh, you won't get *fiancé;* you'll get *fiancÈ.* In general, accented characters don't translate correctly. Other characters that don't translate correctly include em dashes, en dashes, bullets, and quotation marks. Ouch! QuarkConverter solves this problem by "hard-coding" these characters into the XPress Tag file using ASCII numbers. (For example, <\#147> is the QuarkXPress code for an opening quotation mark on the PC.)

That also means the characters won't be lost or converted into something else when the document is saved as an XPress Tag (text) file. For example, on a PC, if you save the copyright symbol, ©, in a text file, you'll get this: (c). Saving a.m. (lowercase letters formatted as small caps) in a text file gives you this: A.M. (capitalized letters, which you'd have to lowercase and reformat in QuarkXPress). Saving curly, "smart" quotation marks gives you straight, "un-smart" ones ("like these").

If you tell it to, QuarkXPress will convert straight quotation marks into curly ones on import, but it won't do it as intelligently as you might like. For example, if you've carefully used apostrophes (as opposed to single quotation marks) at the beginning of such abbreviated words as *'tis, 'twas,* and *'49er,* the distinction will be lost when the document is saved as an XPress Tag (text) file. And when the file is imported into QuarkXPress, the apostrophes will become single opening quotation marks (*'tis, 'twas,* and *'49er*), which you don't want. QuarkConverter solves this problem. The result is that when you fix apostrophes and quotation marks the way you want them in Microsoft Word, they'll stay that way when the document is brought into QuarkXPress.

Fixing typographical problems

In addition, QuarkConverter eliminates various typographical problems with the following options, which you can select:

• Placing discretionary hyphens at the beginning of hyphenated words (except those that begin paragraphs, which would prevent using drop caps on those words) and after all hyphens. This prevents such bad end-of-line breaks as *self-reli-ance.* You never want to break an already broken word, right? I don't, unless doing so makes the line extremely loose, and in that case you can fix it by hand.
• Placing discretionary hyphens at the beginning of words joined by an em dash, and after all em dashes between words. This, too, prevents bad breaks.
• Placing discretionary hyphens at the beginning of contractions, such as couldn't, shouldn't, they're, and so on. (The complete list is couldn't, didn't, doesn't, hadn't, hasn't, isn't, oughtn't, shouldn't, they're, wasn't, we're, wouldn't, and you're.) I thought about putting discretionary hyphens at the beginning of words that end with a liquid l, such as particle and terrible, but the proper way of handling those is to put them into your QuarkXPress hyphenation exception dictionary. QuarkXPress, as of this writing, won't let you include words with apostrophes.
• Placing nonbreaking spaces after the first two periods in a set of ellipses (. . .), and after the first three periods in a set of ellipses followed by a space and then single or double closing quotation marks (. . ."). No more broken ellipses, and your ellipses can be justified, too! You're not using that ugly little ellipses "character" (…), I hope.

Translating index entries

Finally, QuarkConverter translates Word index entries into those for QuarkXPress. This makes it possible for an editor or indexer to create an index in a Word document, using Word's automatic indexing features (or my DEXter or DEXembed programs available at www.editorium.com). When you bring that document into QuarkXPress, the index entries will become Quark index entries, making it possible to generate an index automatically after typesetting and pagination have taken place. This is valuable because editors don't have to worry about indexing in QuarkXPress, and it also saves time in the production process because indexing can take place—in Word—*before* rather than after typesetting and pagination. You may be interested in my DEXter and DexEmbed add-ins for help with this process.

Microsoft Word and QuarkXPress actually handle indexing quite differently, as you might expect. However, enough overlap exists that QuarkConverter supports and will convert the following index functions from Word:

- Main entry.
- Subentry.
- Sub-subentry (follows a colon after a subentry).
- Range of pages (marked with a bookmark). This is actually converted to QuarkXPress's "following number of paragraphs" index entry.
- *See, See also,* and *See herein.*

Please note that if you decide to translate index entries, you *must* manually insert an XPress Tag version code at the top of your document *after* running QuarkConverter and *before* bringing the document into QuarkXPress. QuarkConverter can't do this for you because it has no way of knowing what XPress Tag version you are using. To translate index entries, you must have at least version 2.03, and the code at the beginning of your document would look something like this: <2.03>. To find out what version of XPress Tags you are using, export a document ("Save Text") as an XPress Tag file from QuarkXPress. Then open the file into Microsoft Word. You'll see the version code at the top of the document. This is the code you must type in at the top of the files created by QuarkConverter if you want to use automatic index entries. Please see your QuarkXPress documentation for more information.

Saving files from QuarkConverter

When QuarkConverter is finished, it automatically saves your documents as text files, gives them a .txt extension to differentiate them from your original documents, and places them in the same folder as your original documents. For example, let's say you used QuarkConverter on a document called DOCUMENT.DOC in a folder called FOLDER. When QuarkConverter was finished, you could look in FOLDER and see your original file, DOCUMENT.DOC, along with a new text file, DOCUMENT.TXT, which is the document you would import into QuarkXPress. The .txt extension is to differentiate the converted document from your original one.

Running QuarkConverter

To run QuarkConverter, click the *QuarkConverter* icon on the ribbon. QuarkConverter will present you with options about how you want your documents converted:

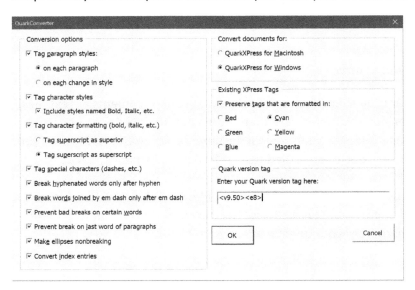

Convert documents for

On the top right, QuarkConverter asks you to select the operating system on which you will be using *QuarkXPress* (not the one on which you're now using QuarkConverter):

- QuarkXPress for Macintosh.
- QuarkXPress for Windows.

Conversion options

On the left, it asks you to select certain conversion options (I recommend using all of these unless you have a good reason not to):

• Tag paragraph styles, either on each paragraph or on each change of style. For purposes of completeness, I prefer each paragraph.

• Tag character styles (with the option to include or exclude character styles named Italic, Bold, Bold Italic, Underline, Strikethrough, Superscript, Subscript, Small Caps, All Caps, and Hidden, which some people use instead of Word's built-in character formatting [bold, italic, etc.]). Please note that if you use this option, character formatting (such as italic) applied *on top of* a character style will be lost.

• Tag character formatting (including bold, italic, underline, strikethrough, superscript, subscript, and raised 3 points). Here you have the option to tag superscript as superior (with the <V> tag) or as superscript (with the <+> tag). Please note that whichever option you choose, formatting raised 3 points will be tagged with the opposite tag (<+> or <V>). Many typesetters prefer the first option (superior), as the second (superscript) may interfere with leading in QuarkXPress.

• Tag special characters (such as dashes, quotation marks, and accented characters).

• Break hyphenated words only after hyphen.

• Break words joined by em dash only after em dash.

• Prevent bad breaks on certain words.

• Prevent breaks on last word of paragraphs.

• Make ellipses nonbreaking.

• Convert index entries.

Existing XPress Tags

If you decide to tag special characters (which you should), QuarkConverter includes angle brackets as some of those characters. If you already have XPress Tags in your document, that's a problem, because XPress Tags start and end with angle brackets. You can get around this by formatting your existing XPress Tags in a color: red, green, blue, cyan, yellow, or magenta. Then QuarkConverter will know that they are XPress Tags and won't tag them as angle brackets—as long as you tell QuarkConverter to preserve existing XPress Tags in the color you've used. This option also preserves colored, straight (uncurly) quotation marks, which are sometimes used in XPress Tags.

There's an easy way to color existing XPress Tags and the information inside them:

1. In Word, Click *Edit > Replace* to bring up the Replace dialog.
2. Enter \<*\> in the Find What box.
3. Enter ^& in the Replace With box.
4. With your cursor still in the Replace With box, click the *Format* button (you may need to click the *More* button before this is available).
5. Click *Font*.
6. Click the color you want to use (red, green, blue, cyan, yellow, or magenta).
7. Click *OK.*
8. Put a check in the box labeled *Use Wildcards.*
9. Click *Replace All* to mark everything in angle brackets in the color you selected. If you want to pick and choose which bracketed material to color, click the *Find Next* button and then the *Replace* button as needed.

Quark version tag

Your XPress Tags file *must* include the version tag as the first thing in the document. The tag should look something like this:

    <v9.50><e8>

To find out what the tag actually is for your version of QuarkXPress, export a document ("Save Text" or "Export Text") as an XPress Tag file from QuarkXPress. Then open the that file into Microsoft Word. You'll see the version code at the top of the document.

You can type the code manually into an XPress Tags document, but a better solution is to enter the code into the QuarkConverter dialog (in the box on the lower right labeled "Quark version tag").

Finishing up

After you've selected the QuarkConverter options you want to use, click *OK*. (If you don't select any options, QuarkConverter won't convert your document.) QuarkConverter will ask which documents you would like it to work on:

- The active document.
- All open documents.
- All documents in a folder.

Choose the option that fits your needs. The documents will be converted based on your options and saved to their original folders as text files with the extension .txt.

Importing XPress Tag files Into QuarkXPress

Importing an XPress Tag file into QuarkXPress is a fairly simple matter. In older versions of the program:

1. Create a new document (or open an existing one) in QuarkXPress.
2. Place your cursor into the document where you want the text to begin.
3. Click the *File* menu.
4. Click *Get Text.*
5. Click *Include Style Sheets.*
6. Find and click the XPress Tag file.
7. Click *OK.*

The XPress Tag file will be imported into the QuarkXPress document, and you can modify the style sheets to match the type specifications the document is supposed to have.

In more recent versions of QuarkXPress (notably Quark 7), you *must* include the version tag at the beginning of the XPress Tag file. If you don't, QuarkXPress won't recognize it as an XPress Tags file and won't give you the option to "Include Style Sheets."

Actually, that option is no longer even called "Include Style Sheets." It's now called "Interpret XPress Tags." Here's the procedure for more recent versions of QuarkXPress:

1. Create a new document (or open an existing one) in QuarkXPress.
2. Place your cursor into the document's text box where you want the text to begin.
3. Click the *File* menu.
4. Click *Import Text.*

5. Click *Interpret XPress Tags.*
6. Find and click the XPress Tag file.
7. Click *OK.*

InDesignConverter

In the past several years, the ability of Adobe InDesign to import Word documents has markedly improved, so you may no longer need InDesignConverter. But if you're having problems bringing Word documents into InDesign, InDesignConverter offers a good solution, translating Microsoft Word documents into InDesign tag files that can be imported into InDesign almost automatically. This also solves several other problems, all of which are explained below.

InDesignConverter saves Word documents as InDesign tagged files that can be imported into InDesign. But doesn't InDesign import Word documents directly? Why would someone use tagged files? Here's why:

• Word documents typically have all kinds of nasty overrides that you'll need to clean up in InDesign. (Tagged files don't.)

• If you "remove styles and formatting from text and tables" when importing, you'll *lose* the styles and formatting (bad). But . . .

• If you "preserve styles and formatting from text and tables," fonts may not translate correctly. For example, InDesign might see Times New Roman as "[Times]." And you'll still get all those overrides.

• InDesign looks for a *separate* italic font if italic (for example) has been applied. If the font doesn't exist (as in a client's Word file), you'll have to specify a font to use. (Just one more step . . .)

- InDesign may complain that a Word document "uses one or more fonts which are not currently available on your system." If it does, InDesign will then "use a substitute font until the original font becomes available." Or (again) you can specify a font to use.

If you get Word documents that are squeaky clean, formatted with styles only, InDesign will generally do a good job of importing them. But how often do you get a Word document that's squeaky clean? Most typesetters and designers get Word documents from all over the place, with all kinds of weird formatting. If you face the same problem, you might want to try importing tag files from InDesignConverter.

InDesign tag files

What are tag files? InDesign tag files are text files that use tags to mark formatting. For example, an InDesign tag file has no italic text. In fact, it can't, since it's just a text file. Instead, it includes the character-style tag <CharStyle:Italic> in front of an italicized word, and when InDesign sees that tag, it turns on italics. Then, when it sees the closing <CharStyle:> tag, it turns italics off. Similarly, an InDesign tag file might include the tag <ParaStyle:Heading 1> in front of a paragraph that will be a main heading. When InDesign sees that tag, it formats the following text with the characteristics the typesetter has specified for Heading 1 in the document's paragraph style with that name.

So how do you get an InDesign tag file? That's where InDesignConverter comes in. InDesignConverter turns Microsoft Word documents into InDesign tag files that can be brought into InDesign, allowing a typesetter to change type specifications globally. For example, let's say you've been editing in Word and have marked spec levels using paragraph styles (which is what you *should* do). You used the style Heading 1 for your main headings and Heading 2 as subheads. When you convert your document with InDesignConverter, those headings will be tagged as <ParaStyle:Heading 1> and

<ParaStyle:Heading 2>. Character styles will be tagged as well. Also, most character *formatting* will be tagged (as characters styles named for the formatting, such as <CharStyle:Italic>), including bold, italic, underline, word underline, strikethrough, small caps, all caps, superscript, subscript, and raised (by 3 points). (Such oddities as shadow, outline, double underline, and dotted underline are not supported and will be lost, unless you change them into something else before using InDesignConverter.)

Note: InDesignConverter does not convert such formatting as fonts, point size, paragraph formatting, kerning, and so on, all of which should be defined in your InDesign styles, not in directly applied formatting.

Note well: None of the styles will have formatting when a tag file is first imported into InDesign. That will probably leave you wondering, "Hey, where'd all my formatting go?" Actually, the fact that there's no formatting is kind of the point, as it allows you (in fact, *requires* you) to *set* the formatting for each style you've imported. For example, if you have a character style named "Italic," you'll need to edit its "basic character formats" to use italic formatting in InDesign, and after you've done so, any text formatted with the Italic character style will (behold!) be automatically displayed in italic. You'll see all the imported styles (with a little floppy disk icon to their right, indicating they've been imported) in InDesign's Paragraph Styles and Character Styles palettes. You can edit a style by right-clicking it and then selecting *Edit.*

However, if you're importing a tag file into an InDesign document that *already has* formatted styles with the *same names* as those you're importing, the text will automatically pick up the proper formatting when it's imported. For this to happen, the import option for "Resolve Text Style Conflicts Using" must be set to "Publication Definition" (which is the default setting).

The InDesign Start File Tag

Please note that your file *must* include an InDesign Start File Tag at the top of your document. Here are a few common options, in decreasing order of desirability. Please see your InDesign documentation for more information. *Note:* "WIN" and "MAC" designate the platform *on which you'll be running InDesign,* not the platform on which you're running the converter.

```
<UNICODE-WIN>
<UNICODE-MAC>
<ANSI-WIN>
<ANSI-MAC>
<ASCII-WIN>
<ASCII-MAC>
```

InDesignConverter will insert the tag for you if you enter it as the first item in the InDesignConverter dialog. Otherwise, InDesign will reject your file (and not import it).

Typographer's quotes and character translation

If you tell it to, InDesign will convert straight quotation marks into curly ones (also known as smart quotes or typographer's quotes) on import, but it won't do it as intelligently as you might like. For example, if you've carefully used apostrophes (as opposed to single quotation marks) in your Word document at the beginning of such abbreviated words as *'tis, 'twas,* and *'49er,* the distinction will be lost when the document is imported into InDesign; the apostrophes will become single quotation marks (*'tis, 'twas,* and *'49er*), which is not what you want.

A better approach is to get the curly quotation marks and apostrophes the way you want them in your Word document. Then turn *off* InDesign's import option to "Use

Typographer's Quotes." The quotation marks and apostrophes will import correctly *if* they were correct in the Word document being imported. Why is that so? Because InDesign knows how to import and use Unicode characters. To take advantage of that fact, InDesignConverter saves its tag files in a Unicode text format (specifically, USC-2 Little-Endian Unicode). That means all kinds of Unicode characters (Greek, Arabic, Chinese, etc.) should import correctly.

Fixing typographical problems

In addition, InDesignConverter eliminates various typographical problems with the following options, which you can select:

*   Placing discretionary hyphens at the beginning of hyphenated words (except those that begin paragraphs, which would prevent using drop caps on those words) and after all hyphens. This prevents such bad end-of-line breaks as *self-reli-ance.* You never want to break an already broken word, right? I don't, unless doing so makes the line extremely loose, and in that case you can fix it by hand.
*   Placing discretionary hyphens at the beginning of words joined by an em dash, and after all em dashes between words. This, too, prevents bad breaks.
*   Placing nonbreaking spaces after the first two periods in a set of ellipses (. . .), and after the first three periods in a set of ellipses followed by a space and then single or double closing quotation marks (. . ."). No more broken ellipses, and your ellipses can be justified, too! You're not using that ugly little ellipses "character" (…), I hope.
*   Placing a discretionary hyphen at the beginning of the last word of each paragraph, preventing the last word from breaking.
*   Adding nonbreaking spaces between numbers and words ("2 Chronicles," "Room 4").

Footnotes and endnotes

InDesign (CS2 and later) supports the uses of automatically numbered footnotes, which can be imported from a Microsoft Word document. However, a tag file can't *have* automatically numbered footnotes because it's a text file. InDesignConverter solves this problem by converting footnotes to text but *tagging* them in such a way that InDesign will recognize and import them as footnotes. In addition, InDesignConverter strips endnotes as text to the end of the document, leaving reference numbers in place.

Index entries

Finally, InDesignConverter translates Word index entries into those for InDesign. This makes it possible for an editor or indexer to create an index in a Word document, using Word's automatic indexing features (hopefully with my DEXter or DEXembed indexing add-ins). When you bring the converted document into InDesign, the index entries will become InDesign index entries, making it possible to generate an index automatically after typesetting and pagination have taken place. This is valuable because editors don't have to worry about indexing in InDesign, and it also saves time in the production process because indexing can take place—in Word—*before* rather than after typesetting and pagination.

Microsoft Word and InDesign actually handle indexing quite differently. However, enough overlap exists that InDesignConverter supports and will convert the following (but no other) index elements from Word:

- Main entry.
- Subentry (follows a colon after a main entry).
- Sub-subentry (follows a colon after a subentry).

- Range of pages (marked with a bookmark in word). This is actually converted to InDesign's "For Next # of Paragraphs" index entry type.
- *See, See also,* and *See herein.*

Saving files from InDesignConverter

When InDesignConverter is finished, it automatically saves your documents as Unicode text files, gives them a .txt extension to differentiate them from your original documents, and places them in the same folder as your original documents. For example, let's say you used InDesignConverter on a document called DOCUMENT.DOC in a folder called FOLDER. When InDesignConverter was finished, you could look in FOLDER and see your original file, DOCUMENT.DOC, along with a new text file, DOCUMENT.TXT, which is the document you would import into InDesign.

Running InDesignConverter

To run InDesignConverter, click the *InDesignConverter* menu at the top of your screen in Microsoft Word. InDesignConverter presents you with options about how you want your document converted (I recommend using all of them unless you have a good reason not to):

After you've selected your options and clicked *OK,* InDesignConverter will ask which documents you would like it to work on:

- The active document.
- All open documents.
- All documents in a folder.

Choose the option that fits your needs. The documents will be converted based on your options and saved to their original folders as text files with the extension .txt.

Importing tag files into InDesign

Importing an InDesign tag file into InDesign is a fairly simple matter:

1. Create a new document and text box (or open an existing one) in InDesign.
2. Select the *Text* cursor and place it in the text box.
3. Click the *File* menu.
4. Click *Place.*
5. Put a check in the *Show Import Options* box.
6. Find and click the InDesign tag file you want to import.
7. Remove the check from the *Use Typographer's Quotes* box.
8. Remove the check from the *Remove Text Formatting* box.
9. Under *Resolve Text Style Conflicts Using,* select *Publication Definition.*
10. Click *OK.*
11. Move your now-"loaded" cursor to the desired location and click the left mouse button.

The InDesign tag file will be imported into the InDesign document, and you can (that is, *must*) edit the document's paragraph and character styles to match the type specifications you want it to have.

Projects

Save open documents as a project

Open documents saved as a project

Close documents saved as a project

Delete a project

Merge open documents

Projects provides a way to save and open all the Microsoft Word documents related to a project. For example, let's say you're editing (or writing!) a 3,000-page fantasy trilogy along the lines of *Harry Potter*. For each volume, you have the chapters themselves, plot outlines, scene lists, character profiles, maps, notes, and much more, all organized in various folders. While working, you keep several of these documents open at the same time—for example, all of the documents related to chapter 23. Using the Projects feature, you can save those documents as a named project ("Chapter 23 Documents," for example). Then the next time you need to work on chapter 23, you simply call up that project, which automatically opens all the associated documents in Word.

You can also merge those open documents into one document, and you can close or delete a project after you've finished working on it. Note that deleting a project does *not* delete the files associated with the project; it simply deletes their association *as* a project.

Research

The Research feature includes two different ways to look things up, *Lookups* and *Reference Library.* These are independent of and quite different from Microsoft Word's "research" features. *Lookups* actually looks up selected words for you online. *Reference Library* simply *opens* various online reference works, with an emphasis on style guides for editing.

Lookups

Lookups looks up the currently selected text in online dictionaries, encyclopedias, and other reference works. If text is not selected, Lookups selects and looks up the current word. Choose the reference work you want to use and click OK.

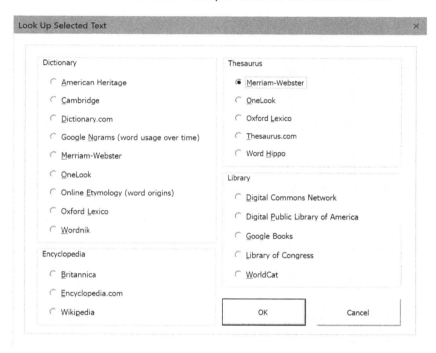

The program remembers the reference work you last used, so if Merriam-Webster is your favorite dictionary, it will already be selected the next time you use Lookups, and you can instantly look up a new word by clicking OK or hitting the ENTER key.

To use Lookups from the keyboard, press CTRL SHIFT F3.

Reference library

Reference library opens a curated selection of online reference works, including editorial style guides, encyclopedias, and much more. It remembers the last reference work you used, so if *Chicago* is your favorite style guide, it will already be selected the next time you use Reference Library.

To use Reference Library from the keyboard, press CTRL SHIFT F4.

MacroVault

1 TurnOnCurlyQuotes

2 TestPandocGet

3 Shakespeare2LyX

4 PrepareModernPlays

5 CleanSpeaker

6 RemoveReturnBeforeActs

7 SeparatePlayerNames

8 ConvertHeadingStyles

MacroVault automatically creates a menu for your own collection of macros—those stored in the NewMacros module of your Normal template (Normal.dotm), which is Word's default location for macros that you have recorded, found, or created.

Making your macros easily accessible is difficult in Word; Editor's ToolKit Plus does it for you. Just click the MacroVault icon to display a list of your macros. To run one of the macros, click it.

Setting the MacroVault keyboard shortcuts

To the left of the macros on the menu, you'll see a list of numbers and letters. Those numbers and letters can be automatically assigned as shortcut keys to the corresponding macros when you hold down ALT CTRL SHIFT. For example, to run the macro labeled "B," you would hold down ALT CTRL SHIFT and press the B key on your keyboard. (You can do this only when the MacroVault menu is no longer showing.) To assign the MacroVault shortcut keys, click *Editor's ToolKit Plus > Set MacroVault keyboard shortcuts.*

Controlling the display of macros in MacroVault

All well and good, "but," you say, I have more than a hundred macros. I don't want them all listed on the MacroVault menu—just the ones I use the most." No problem. If you create a macro called "EndMacroVault," only the macros *above* that macro will be listed in MacroVault. For example, let's say you have the following macros:

```
Sub MyMacro1()
'Macro code goes here
End Sub

Sub MyMacro2()
'Macro code goes here
End Sub
```

```
Sub MyMacro3()
'Macro code goes here
End Sub
```

Let's further suppose that you want only the first two macros to appear on the *MacroVault* menu. You would create a macro called "EndMacroVault" and place it after the first two macros, like this:

```
Sub MyMacro1()
'Macro code goes here
End Sub

Sub MyMacro2()
'Macro code goes here
End Sub

Sub EndMacroVault()
'You don't need anything here.
End Sub

Sub MyMacro3()
'Macro code goes here
End Sub
```

That's it; now only the first two macros will appear on the *MacroVault* menu.

When you run a macro from MacroVault, Editor's ToolKit Plus presents the option to run the macro on the active document, all open documents, or all documents in a folder. As with other batch processes, it also lets you choose which parts of a document to use and how to track revisions.

This brings a great deal of power and flexibility to macros that you've created yourself or found online. Unfortunately, it also brings added danger if something goes wrong, so please, before using this feature, *make sure* your macros do exactly what you want them to. You don't want to run them on a whole folder full of documents, only to find out they've done something you didn't want them to do. As always, *back up your documents* before using, just in case.

Caution: Keep in mind that MacroVault can run on multiple documents, so if some of your macros *include* opening, closing, or switching documents, you'll need to be especially careful about keeping those operations in their proper order. In fact, I'd recommend not using MacroVault with macros that do things like that. The same is true for macros that turn revision tracking on or off, as this is controlled by the option you set for revision tracking when doing batch processing.

NOTE: MacroVault works on documents *as a whole.* It does *not* work on a single word, line, or paragraph, or on a selection of text. If you have a macro that *does* work on one of those things, please *don't* try to use it with MacroVault. Instead, place it on Word's Quick Access Toolbar (QAT) for easy access.

Registration

If you like Editor's ToolKit Plus and plan to continue using it, you must purchase a license to do so. If you don't, your copy of the program is for evaluation purposes only, and it will stop working after 45 days. After you purchase a license to use the program, you'll automatically receive a password (by email) that will unlock the program to run without limitation on time or use.

The terms of your license prohibit you from giving your program password to someone else or using it on someone else's computer. However, you may use the password for your own use on up to *three* computers. For example, you could install Editor's ToolKit Plus and use your password on your computer at work, your computer at home, and your laptop. However, you may actually *run* the program on only one of your computers at a time. If you need to run the program on more than one computer at a time (for example, for concurrent use by a family member or employee), you must purchase another license and get another password for the program. This is the honest and legal thing to do. Besides that, the Editorium is a *very* small business that needs your support. Thanks for your cooperation.

Getting a password

Here's how to purchase a program license so you can get your password:

1.   Go to http://www.editorium.com/register.htm and click Editor's ToolKit Plus. Or, in Word, just click Editor's ToolKit Plus > Register Editor's ToolKit Plus > Purchase Editor's ToolKit Plus.

2.   Follow the online instructions.

You'll receive your password automatically by return email as soon as your payment is processed. If you're paying by credit card, you'll receive your password almost immediately. Just check your email as soon as your online registration is complete.

Using your password

Once you've received your password from the Editorium, you'll need to enter it into the Editor's ToolKit Plus program. To do so, click *Editor's ToolKit Plus > Register Editor's ToolKit Plus.* The Registration dialog will appear on your screen.

Carefully type (or, better, paste) the password into the box labeled "Please enter your password/ registration code." Then click the *OK* button.

If you have a valid password and enter it correctly, the program will tell you that your registration was successful. After that, the program will run without limitation on time or use.

Questions?

I hope you find Editor's ToolKit Plus to be immensely useful. If you have questions, comments, or thoughts about how it could be improved, please let me know.

> support@editorium.com
> www.editorium.com

The Editorium provides word-processing tools for editors, writers, indexers, typesetters, and other publishing professionals. You can download fully functioning evaluation copies of these tools free of charge from the Editorium's site on the World Wide Web at www.editorium.com.

Appendix 1: Keyboard Shortcuts

Editing

Insert	Extend Selection
ALT Backspace	Delete to Start of Word
ALT Delete	Delete to End of Word
ALT CTRL End	Delete to End of Line
ALT CTRL Home	Delete to Start of Line
CTRL SHIFT E	Copy selected text and open editorial style sheet

Inserting bookmarks

CTRL 1 (2, 3, etc.)	Set Bookmark1 (2, 3, etc.)
ALT CTRL 1 (2, 3, etc.)	Go to Bookmark1 (2, 3, etc.)

Inserting special characters

SHIFT F2	Em Dash
SHIFT F3	En Dash
SHIFT F4	Bullet (followed by a tab)

Reviewing revisions

ALT CTRL SHIFT Right Arrow	Next Revision
ALT CTRL SHIFT Left Arrow	Previous Revision
ALT CTRL SHIFT Up Arrow	Retain Revision
ALT CTRL SHIFT Down Arrow	Remove Revision

Applying heading and other styles

CTRL SHIFT N	Normal Style
CTRL SHIFT B	AutoStyle Block Quote
CTRL SHIFT L	AutoStyle List
CTRL SHIFT P	AutoStyle Poem
CTRL SHIFT 1	Apply Heading 1
CTRL SHIFT 2	Apply Heading 2
CTRL SHIFT 3	Apply Heading 3

CTRL SHIFT 4	Apply Heading 4
CTRL SHIFT 5	Apply Heading 5
CTRL SHIFT 6	Apply Heading 6
CTRL SHIFT 7	Apply Heading 7
CTRL SHIFT 8	Apply Heading 8
CTRL SHIFT 9	Apply Heading 9

Applying character styles (see "Set character style keyboard shortcuts")

CTRL B	Bold (toggle)
CTRL I	Italic (toggle)
CTRL U	Underline (toggle)
CTRL /	Strikethrough (toggle)
F6	Small caps (toggle)
CTRL +	Subscript (toggle)
CTRL SHIFT +	Superscript (toggle)

Applying ListFixer styles

ALT SHIFT B	Apply fixed bullets styled
ALT SHIFT N	Apply fixed numbers styled

After performing a Find/Replace operation

ALT CTRL SHIFT >	Find again forward
ALT CTRL SHIFT <	Find again backward
ALT CTRL SHIFT /	Replace

Function keys (see the ETKPlus 2023 keyboard template)

F1	Microsoft Word help
F2	Mark Revisions (toggle)
F3	Stet Revisions
F4	Show Revisions (toggle)
F5	Styles
F6	Small Caps (toggle)
F7	Italic (toggle)
F8	Make Word Italic or Roman (toggle)
F9	Capitalize Word
F10	Lowercase Word
F11	Transpose Words
F12	Transpose Characters
SHIFT F1	Reveal Formatting task pane (toggle)

SHIFT F2	Em Dash
SHIFT F3	En Dash
SHIFT F4	Bullet
SHIFT F5	Find
SHIFT F6	Replace
SHIFT F7	Spelling
SHIFT F8	Thesaurus
SHIFT F9	Go To
SHIFT F10	Go Back
SHIFT F11	Mark Editing Place
SHIFT F12	Find Editing Place
CTRL F1	Extend Selection
CTRL F2	Cut
CTRL F3	Copy
CTRL F4	Paste
CTRL F5	Cut to Spike
ALT CTRL F5	Copy to Spike
CTRL F6	Insert Spike

CTRL F7	AutoCorrect
CTRL F8	AutoText
CTRL F9	Insert Footnote
CTRL F10	View Footnotes (toggle)
CTRL F11	Insert Comment
CTRL F12	View Comments (toggle)
CTRL SHIFT F1	Hide Ribbon (toggle)
CTRL SHIFT F2	Switcheroo
CTRL SHIFT F3	Lookups
CTRL SHIFT F4	Reference Library
CTRL SHIFT F5	Arrange Documents (toggle)
CTRL SHIFT F6	Next Window
CTRL SHIFT F7	Split Window (toggle)
CTRL SHIFT F8	Other Pane
CTRL SHIFT F9	View Draft
CTRL SHIFT F10	View Print Layout
CTRL SHIFT F11	View Outline
CTRL SHIFT F12	Activate Cockpit (toggle)

Appendix 2: Word Functions for Editors

Here are some Word functions with which you should be thoroughly familiar if you're editing in Word. Please consult your Word manual and Help file for information on these topics.

- Annotations (Comments)
- AutoCorrect
- AutoFormat
- AutoText
- Bookmarks
- Change Case
- Character Formats (italic, bold, and so on)
- Cross-References
- Document Properties
- Draft View
- Find
- Font
- Full Screen
- Go Back
- Go To

- Grammar
- Index
- Insert
- New Window
- Normal, Outline, Print, and Master Document Views
- Notes
- Options
- Paragraph Formats (centered, justified, and so on)
- Protect Document
- Quick Access Toolbar (QAT)
- Redo
- Replace
- Revisions
- Save As (including file conversions)
- Show All
- Sort Text
- Spell
- Spike
- Style Gallery
- Styles
- Symbols
- Tables
- Templates
- Thesaurus
- Undo

Of course, you should also understand such basic functions as opening, closing, and saving documents; manipulating windows; moving around and among documents; and entering, selecting, deleting, cutting, copying, and pasting text.

Terms of Agreement

By using Editor's ToolKit Plus, you agree to these terms:

LICENSE AGREEMENT

The Editor's ToolKit Plus software and its documentation (collectively the Software) are protected by the United States copyright laws and international treaties and are owned solely and entirely by the Editorium (the licensor).

You (the licensee) may install the Software for your own use on up to THREE computers (for example, at work, at home, and on a laptop). You may evaluate the Software at no charge for up to 45 days. After that, you must purchase a license to continue using the Software.

You may freely transfer copies of the Software to others for evaluation. You may NOT let someone else use your password for the Software or rent or lease your license to run it, but you may transfer the license to someone else who accepts this agreement.

You may not modify, reverse engineer, decompile, disassemble, unencrypt, or create derivative works from the Software. You may not use the Software in any manner that infringes the intellectual property or other rights of another party. You may not copy or sell the Software for commercial gain.

DISCLAIMER OF WARRANTY AND LIABILITY

The Editorium disclaims all warranties on the Software, expressed or implied, including but not limited to warranties of merchantability and fitness for any particular application, use, or purpose. You use it at your own risk. Under no circumstances, including its own negligence, shall the Editorium or its suppliers be liable for any special, incidental, or consequential damages or loss that result from the use of, or the inability to use, the Software.

This agreement shall be construed, interpreted, and governed by the laws of the State of Utah in the United States of America.

INDEX

www.ingramcontent.com/pod-product-compliance
Lightning Source LLC
Chambersburg PA
CBHW080407060326

40689CB00019B/4156